Joy and Sorrow
SONGS OF ANCIENT CHINA

Joy and Sorrow
SONGS OF ANCIENT CHINA

A New Translation of
SHI JING GUO FENG

by Ha Poong Kim

sussex
ACADEMIC
PRESS
Brighton • Chicago • Toronto

2 4 6 8 10 9 7 5 3 1

First published in Great Britain in 2016 by
SUSSEX ACADEMIC PRESS
PO Box 139, Eastbourne BN24 9BP

Distributed in North America by
SUSSEX ACADEMIC PRESS
Independent Publishers Group
814 N Franklin St, Chicago, IL 60610, USA

British Library Cataloguing in Publication Data
A CIP catalogue record for this book is available from the British Library.

Library of Congress Cataloging-in-Publication Data
Names: Kim, Ha Poong, 1928– translator.
Title: Joy and sorrow : Songs of ancient China : a new translation of Shi Jing Guo Feng : a
Chinese–English bilingual edition / Ha Poong Kim.
Other titles: Shi jing. Guo feng. English & Chinese. | Songs of ancient China: a new
translation of Shi Jing Guo Feng: a Chinese–English bilingual edition
Description: Chicago : Sussex Academic Press, 2016. | "First published in 2016 in Great
Britain . and in the United States of America by Sussex Academic Press . . ." | Includes
bibliographical references.
Identifiers: LCCN 2015042602 (print) | LCCN 2015048272 (ebook) |
ISBN 9781845197926 (pb : alk. paper) | ISBN 9781782842989 (e-pub) |
ISBN 9781782842996 (mobi) | ISBN 9781782843009 (pdf)
Classification: LCC PL2478 .F49 2016 (print) | LCC PL2478 (ebook) |
DDC 895.11/108dc—23
LC record available at http://lccn.loc.gov/2015042602

Typeset & designed by Sussex Academic Press, Brighton & Eastbourne.
Printed and bound by CPI Group (UK) Ltd, Croydon, CR0 4YY

Contents

CONTENTS

Preface

The *Shi Jing* is the oldest anthology of Chinese songs. It contains 305 songs of ancient China, the 12th–7th century BCE. The collection is divided into four parts: *Guo Feng* (160 songs), *Xiao Ya* (74 songs), *Da Ya* (31 songs), and *Song* (40 songs). The present work is a translation of the first of these four parts, namely *Guo Feng*, which means "songs of various states" within the Zhou kingdom (1122–255 BCE). The word *feng* by itself refers to the local custom of a particular region, so that most of the songs in this part may be regarded as folksongs or ballads, sung by the common people of a given state. Unlike these songs, those in the other three parts are generally believed to have been composed for various occasions of celebration and worship (such as royal banquets and rites of sacrifice), so that they typically sing the great achievements of the fore-fathers of the Zhou house, invoke blessings for the king and his descendants, and at times give even admonitions for his future succes-sors. In this respect, they are clearly dynastic songs, which often refer to the dynastic legends.

The songs included in this translation, on the other hand, have mostly a more spontaneous origin: they were born wild, so to speak. They were born wild in that northeastern part of China along the Yellow River where the present-day Xian and Loyang region would occupy the central part. That is, they were the spontaneous voices of the ancient people of China who lived even before Confucius was born. I note this fact espe-cially because the Chinese civilization as we know it today is fundamentally Confucian. In this sense, one may say that these voices are the songs of joy and sorrow sung by those Chinese people whose world was very different from the Confucian universe, with which we tend to identify Chinese civilization.[1]

This is of course not to suggest that the rich history of Chinese poetry that was to come had little to do with the *Shi Jing*. Historically, indeed, this anthology was to become one of the two ancestors of the poetic tradition of China, along with its later counterpart *Chu Ci*, which contains the poems by several poets from the South, most importantly the long poems by Qu Yuan (340–278 BCE), the first known poet of China.

To be sure, the text of the *Shi Jing*[2] comes down to us in our familiar Chinese characters. But few, even Chinese people of today, can read it without commentaries, especially the songs in *Guo Feng*. For what one sees in the text are merely the written versions of the songs, which were originally *sung* or orally cited in ancient Chinese, some possibly more than four centuries before Confucius (551–479 BCE). In fact, the language of the *Shi Jing* was considered "old" Chinese (*gu wen*) already during the Han period (206 BCE–25 CE), when the first commentaries on this anthology appeared. Perhaps one may explain their appearance in view of the difficulty of reading the text. But one may recognize also a more fundamental reason for this.

It was during the reign of Wu-di (Emperor Wu) (140–87 BCE) of the Han dynasty that there appeared the so-called "three schools of *Shi* studies," each giving its own interpretation of the *Shi Jing*. These schools are believed to have produced each their own commentaries on this classic, though no text has survived to tell us of their interpretations. Importantly, Wu-di was the first ruler of China who made Confucianism the state ideology, favoring it over all the other philosophical schools. With the ascendance of Confucianism came the growing importance of the studies of the Confucian canon, which includes the *Shi Jing*. Here we can see the external circumstance in which the three *Shi* schools came into existence—namely, the political circumstance in which the Confucian commentaries on this difficult text began to appear, the condition never to abate for nearly two millennia.

The text of the *Shi Jing* in the present form is often called *Mao Shi*, because it was the text contained in a commentary written by a certain Mao Heng[3], of whom little is known, except that the work appeared about the same period during which the three *Shi* schools were active. One common characteristic of the songs of the *Shi Jing* is that as a rule each line consists of four characters, hence four syllables. This simple form was later replaced by five- or seven-character lines during the Han period. There is, however, another common characteristic of these songs, which was to become a distinct aspect of Chinese poetic tradition. The reader of this collection will notice that most songs begin with a line or lines referring to, or descriptive of, a certain natural phenomenon, such as tree, flower, bird, mountain, river, season, and the like. One finds typically such a beginning in later Chinese poems.

About three centuries after the appearance of the *Mao Shi*, the great Confucian scholar Zheng Xuan (127–200), of Later Han, added his own comments to Mao's, and this new version quickly established itself as the most authoritative commentary on the *Shi Jing*. This work by Zheng is commonly called the "Old Commentary" (*Gu Zhu*), to be distinguished from the "New Commentary" (*Xin Zhu*), the work by another great Confucian scholar (of Neo-Confucianism), Zhu Xi (1130–1200), of the Song period. Perhaps one can safely say that these two commentaries together have dominated the common reception of the *Shi Jing* until today, which amounts to the reading of those pre-Confucian songs fundamentally in a Confucian perspective.[4]

In my translation of this anthology, I have consulted a number of recent Japanese works on it. With the exception of one commentator/translator, I have found they all follow fundamentally the traditional way of reading the ancient songs in light of the Zheng Xuan's and Zhu Xi's commentaries. The exception is the late professor Shirakawa Shizuka, an authority in the studies of ancient China. She wrote several works on the *Shi Jing*, including her translation (1990) of its first part, *Guo Feng*, the very part this book translates. Calling her approach ethnographical, she eschews the traditional Confucian reading—that is, any allegorical or moralistic reading—of the many love songs of this part; instead, she reads them simply as such,[5] often interpreting them in view of the ancient festivals. In such instances, I generally follow her interpretation.

I would not call my approach ethnographical or ethnological. Generally, I read the songs in *Guo Feng* as spontaneous expressions of the simple folks of ancient China—their voices of joy and sorrow in the vicissitude of human existence. Of course, theirs were not abstract voices: they were voices uttered in the ancient world of China, the culture so different even from what we know today by Chinese civilization. My notes and the following Introduction are intended to help the reader hear their voices in *their* world.

Finally, I would like to acknowledge my indebtedness to the poet Elena Georgiou for her editing of this work. I thank her.

Ha Poong Kim

Note on Spelling and Pronunciation of Romanized Chinese

This book uses the Romanizing system of Chinese called *Pinyin*. Some
of the rules of spelling and pronunciation are quite different from the
ways in which English words are normally spelled and expected to sound.
The following short list of spelling may help those unfamiliar with the
system come close to the original sounds of certain Chinese consonants.

c   =   *ts* as in ten*ts*
ch =   *ch* as in *ch*irp
j   =   *j* as in *j*eep
q   =   *ch* as in *ch*eese
x   =   *sh* as in *sh*oe (very soft, nearly voiceless)
z   =   *ds* as in li*ds*
zh =   *j* as in *j*erk

Notes to the Preface

1 Here, of course, I am not suggesting that Confucius's teachings had little
   to do with the culture and tradition into which he was born. In fact, in one
   of his sayings he declares: "I transmit and invent nothing. I am faithful to
   and love the old way. . . ." (*Analects*, Ch. 7). But see Appendix.
2 The *Shi Jing* has been given in English various titles such as *The Book of
   Poetry*, *The Confucian Odes*, and *The Book of Songs*. In the title, *Shi* means the
   text of a song, and *Jing* scripture or classic. Originally, the anthology was
   simply called *Shi*, as Confucius referred to it in the *Analects*.
3 Or Mao Chang? Or, possibly, both.
4 During the middle part of the Qing period, a number of scholars tried to
   give a new interpretation of the *Shi Jing* on the basis of their philological
   studies of ancient Chinese. However, such a scholarly effort didn't really
   change the centuries-old way of reading the text in the Confucian way.
5 As far as I know, it was Marcel Granet, the French ethnographer, who first
   recognized the songs of *Guo Feng* as "popular songs" or love songs, and
   treated them as such in his *Fête et chansons anciennes de la Chine* (1919),
   rejecting the traditional interpretations by the Chinese commentators.
   Shirakawa introduces and discusses Granet's ethnographical approach and
   acknowledges her indebtedness to him in her two works on the *Shi Jing* (*Shi
   Kyō* and *Shi Kyō Kokufū*), though she does question the accuracy of many
   of Granet's translations. Arthur Waley also writes that Granet was the first
   scholar to realize "the true nature of the poems," but adds that he "differs
   from M. Granet as regards some general questions and many details" (*The*

Book of Songs, p. 317). I agree with both authors on the epoch-making contribution of Granet to the interpretation of the *Shi Jing*, while finding many of his translations again problematic, as they do. It may be noted that in his work Granet gives his translations of over fifty songs, primarily *in support of* his three ethnographical themes: "rustic themes," "village loves," and "songs of the rivers and mountains" in ancient China. In these themes he sees "what the love-songs, even when personal, have preserved of the primitive art of the song" (E. D. Edwards, trans., *Festivals and Songs of Ancient China*, p. 31). Perhaps only by philological or rather archeological works can we bring to light the original, native meaning of these ancient songs, by removing the Confucian debris that have collected over them for centuries.

Introduction
Confucius and the Confucians on the *Shi*

1.

In the Preface, I referred to the Confucian reading of the *Shi Jing*. Does this mean that Confucius himself read it in the way those later commentators read it? The answer is no. How did the Master read it? And why did he so often urge his pupils to study it? What was his attitude toward it?

In his brief biography of Confucius in *Records of the Historian* (*Shi Ji*, 17) Si-ma Qian (145–86?) writes that Confucius selected from a collection of over 3000 songs (*shi*) those which he found "in conformity with the rules of propriety" (*li yi*), arranged 305 of them in their present order, and sang them over musical accompaniment. On the basis of this record, it is customary to regard him as the compiler of the *Shi Jing*. While one may question this attribution, Confucius's appreciative love of the *Shi*[1] as well as his recognition of its value in the education of a noble man is quite evident in his many sayings in the *Analects*. Let us cite some of them.

(1) Were I to cover the three hundred songs of the *Shi* with one phrase, I would say "thought free of depravity." (II, 2)

(2) "*Guan Guan*, Ospreys"[2] is a song of joy free of debauch, sorrow free of hurt. (III, 20)

(3) When the music master Zhi came to the climax of "*Guan Guan*, Ospreys," *yang yang*, his music flooded my ears! (VIII, 15)

(4) One rises by the *Shi*, stands right by the *Li* [rules of propriety], and fulfills humanness by the *Yue* [music]. (VIII, 8)

(5) After my return to Lu from Wei, I have put the Music (*yue*) in order, so that the *Ya* and the *Song* [of the *Shi*] found their proper places. (IX, 14)

(6) Suppose a man is able to recite by heart the three hundred songs

of the *Shi*. But when given a job in the government, he cannot fulfill it, or when sent abroad on a mission, he is unable to negotiate on his own. If so, of what use would his knowledge of the songs be, even if it were great? (XIII, 5)

(7) [To Boyu, Confucius's son:] Unless you study the *Shi*, you will be at a loss in conversation. (XVI, 13)

(8) [To Boyu:] Have you worked on Zhou Nan and Shao Nan[3]? A man who has not worked on Zhou Nan and Shao Nan is like one who faces up against a wall. (XVII, 10)

(9) Little ones, why is it that you don't study the *Shi*? By the *Shi*, you may arouse people, observe their feelings, associate with them in harmony, and express your grievances. You may use it at home in the service of your father, and abroad in the service of your prince. From it you will come to know the names of many birds, animals, plants and trees. (XVII, 9)

I find the first of these sayings most remarkable: It sums up Confucius's aesthetic sensitivity to the songs of the *Shi*. Why does he love the songs? Because he perceives in them the beauty of human feelings "free of depravity." His comment on "*Guan Guan*, Ospreys" clearly expresses his aesthetic enjoyment of it, "joy free of debauch, sorrow free of pain." It is a very well-known fact that Confucius was a great lover of music. Indeed, he was above all an aesthetic man.[4] One saying reports: "When the Master was visiting Qi, he heard the music of Shao and forgot the taste of meat for three months. He said, 'I never imagined that the playing of any music would reach such perfection'" (VII, 13). It wouldn't be a surprise to hear his remark on Master Zhi's performance of the music of "*Guan Guan*, Ospreys."

In sayings (4)–(5), we may recognize the place of the *Shi* in Confucius's universe. For him the beginning of humanity is proper human sentiments; without them a human being is hardly different from wild animals. Confucius recognizes in the *Shi* the expression of such proper sentiments. Hence, he says, "One rises by the *Shi*." By saying one "stands right by the *Li*," he is referring to the *correct* way of life through observance of the *Li*. But for him it is not the *Li*, but the *Yue* (music) that brings fulfillment to the noble man. It may be noted that when Confucius speaks of the *Yue*, it is not an abstract general concept of music but the existing world of music that he found in his own time, the world which included the songs of the *Shi*. Saying (5) indicates this; here he is referring to the *Ya* and the *Song* of the *Shi*.

In the remaining sayings, (6–9), Confucius tells us how the knowledge of the *Shi* might benefit us in our practical life, not only at home and in association with others but also in government service. How? By *proper use* of the songs in communication, in today's parlance. Knowledge of these songs may enable one to communicate one's thoughts in accordance with the rules of propriety (*li*), without violating one's relation with the interlocutor, whether speaking to one's father or a prince. That is, the songs may be used allegorically,[5] for instance, even for purposes of polite criticism or satire. (One can find instances of allegorical or metaphorical use of particular songs in the *Analects*.) For Confucius, of course, such use of the songs would presuppose the common universe in which both the user and interlocutor appreciate the beauty or value of the songs themselves.[6]

In this respect, saying (6) is particularly interesting. It clearly indicates that the studying of the songs does not mean simply acquiring the ability to retain and recite them. But does the saying also imply that the study of the *Shi* is wasted unless it makes one perform successfully the sort of functions mentioned in it? Of course not. For we have seen Confucius's recognition of the *intrinsic* value of the songs as the expression of human sentiments. For him, indeed, the cultivation of such sentiments is nothing less than the foundation of the noble man's learning, and he urges his pupils to study the *Shi*, above all, for this purpose. By stressing the utility of the study of these songs, he is not denying this more fundamental reason for studying the *Shi*. I point this out here because this fact is all but lost for those Confucian commentators, who tried to read the *Shi Jing* in view of its allegorical meaning or didactic use. Thus, I believe Confucius's reading of the *Shi* was radically different from that of these Confucian scholars, who came after him: his was an aesthetic reading, whereas theirs was either political or moralistic.

2.

Earlier we saw Confucius comment on the first song of the *Shi Jing*: "'*Guan Guan,* Ospreys', in it you hear joy free of debauch and sorrow free of hurt." Let us cite this song in full, before we look at the comments one finds in the standard commentaries ("Old Commentary" and the "New Commentary").

Guan, guan, cry the ospreys
On the isle of the river.
Lovely is this fine maiden,
Fit match for a nobleman.

Long and short grow water mallows,
Left and right, she seeks them.
Lovely is this fine maiden,
Day and night, you seek her.

You seek her but don't get her,
Day and night you think of her.
How sad! How sad!
Turning and tossing on your side.

Long and short grow water mallows,
Left and right, she gathers them.
Lovely is this fine maiden,
Play *qin se*, let us befriend her.

Long and short grow water mallows,
Left and right, she chooses them.
Lovely is this fine maiden,
Beat *zhong gu*, let us delight her.

The "Old Commentary" (*Mao Shi*) has a lengthy preface to this first song, in which it views "*Guan Guan*, Ospreys" as a song praising "the extraordinary virtue of the wife of King Wen," and goes on to state:

> She rejoices at finding a fine maiden to be a companion of the lord. Her concern is to let him find a wise person. Nothing wanton in the maiden's face, and her graceful beauty so appealing, she perceives her wise nature. Thus she feels no jealousy at her goodness. This is the meaning of "*Guan Guan*, Ospreys." (*Mao Xu*)

Zhu Xi's comment in his "New Commentary":

King Wen, a sage by birth, got the wise daughter of the Yi clan and took her as his wife. At her arrival, the people of the court recognized her quiet virtue of profundity, and sang this poem. (*Shi Ji Chuan*)

Clearly in these two comments, the two scholars are not expressing their feelings about the song itself. Rather, Mao is describing it as a song that adores the noble virtue of a wise lady, while Zhu is stating the circumstance in which the song was sung. How different these comments are from Confucius's exclamation, "joy free of debauch and sorrow free of hurt." Of course, neither Mao nor Zhu gives any supporting ground for their assertion. (Their scholarly authority must simply be accepted by any student of the text!) Perhaps, these comments show the underlying purpose of both commentaries, which is to tell the reader how they should be read in Confucian terms, whether in view of the selfless virtue of the King's wife or her quiet virtue of profundity. Why such commentaries? In this particular instance, one reads a song of a simple mallow-picking girl. The student of Confucianism may indeed wonder why the Master has included such a simple song in his collection of songs. Hence, the need for some sort of explanation acceptable in a Confucian perspective, whether in historical or moral terms. These Confucian scholars were to meet this crucial need by giving an allegorical or moralistic reading of the text.

The problem is, however, that such explanations would have little to do with the reading of any given song *as a song*. In the case of "*Guan Guan*, Ospreys," for instance, it has its particular imagery, the very quality which moved the Master to remark "joy free of debauch and sorrow free of hurt." But when the song is to be understood only as an allegory of this or that virtue, such a quality is altogether ignored or at best considered secondary, for now the question shifts from the song to something else, namely its meaning especially in view of Confucian teachings. When "*Guan Guan*, Ospreys" is read as an allegory of a female virtue, one may find oneself asking what aspect of the female virtue does the song represent allegorically, that is, through its image? The absence of jealousy? Calm profundity? This indeed suggests a fundamental problem with this kind of allegorical reading.

For such a reading takes the reader's attention away from the concrete *image* of the song to some abstract *idea* of which the song is supposed to be a mere allegorical representation. In fact, this seems to have been precisely what happened when our Confucian commentators occupied themselves with such an allegorical reading of the songs of the *Shi Jing*. They were no longer interested in the imagery or beauty of a given song itself. But *this* was precisely what prompted the Master to say: "'*Guan Guan*, Ospreys' is a song of joy free of debauch, sorrow free of hurt," and, on another occasion, to admire the music master Zhi's playing by saying, "*Guan Guan*, Ospreys," *yang yang*, his music flooded my ears!" Confucius wasn't referring to anything beyond the song.

Love songs abound in *Guo Feng*, the first part of the *Shi Jing*, which this book translates. But our commentators give them mostly allegorical or moralistic readings. Below I cite as a further example their brief comments on the following song, "Please, Zhongzi".

Please, Zhongzi,
Don't climb over the village wall,
Don't break the willow-trees we have planted.
Not that I am concerned with them,
I am afraid of my parents.
I love you, Zhongzi,
But I am afraid
Of what my parents will say.

Please, Zhongzi,
Don't climb over our fence,
Don't break the mulberry-trees we have planted.
Not that I am concerned with them,
I am afraid of my brothers.
I love you, Zhonzi,
But I am afraid
Of what my brothers will say.

Please, Zhongzi,
Don't climb into our garden,
Don't break the spindle trees we have planted.
Not that I am concerned with them,
I am afraid of what people say.
I love you, Zhongzi,

But I am afraid
Of what people will say.

On this song, which is unmistakably a love song, Mao comments:
"'Please, Zhongzi' is a satire criticizing Duke Zhuang of Zheng, who
hated his mother and attacked his brother. . . ." (*Mao Xu*), while Zhu
simply declares: "This is a song by a licentious woman" (*Shi Ji Chuan*).

3.

An historical note. I have already stated that Mao's commentary ("Old
Commentary") appeared first during the early Han period, and Zheng
Xuan of Later Han added his own comments to it a few centuries later.
Zhu's commentary ("New Commentary") came during the thirteenth
century. And these two works together became the standard sources of
the *Shi Jing* studies for centuries. In view of their questionable
approaches, the reader may wonder why no other school of interpretation
emerged to challenge them during all those years.[7] Of course, this fact
had much to do with predominance of Confucianism as the state ideology
ever since the Wu-di's time. But there was a more definite historical
factor to which one may put a finger: namely, a socio-political circumstance, which made it all but impossible for the emerging of a new school
of interpretation. I am referring to the way the successive dynasties since
the Han recruited their government officials, favoring the students of
Confucianism over all other schools.

We see an early development of competitive examinations for the
choice of government officials during Wu-di's reign. He instituted a
higher institution at the capital for the training of future officials and
encouraged the local districts to build schools. What is known as the
civil examination system did not come until the Sui dynasty (589–618).
Once introduced, however, the system continued to grow and expand as
the single important means of recruiting government officials until the
Qing, the last dynasty, which abolished it only in 1905, six years before
its final collapse last century. What were the subjects of these examinations? They were primarily Confucian texts at every level. At the higher
levels, poetry composition was required, along with knowledge of the
Confucian canon, including the *Shi Jing*.

Now, let us keep in mind that we are speaking of those times in China
when government service was the only prestigious profession any ambi-

tious young man would seek as a career. Therefore practically every intelligent young man was expected to pursue the course of education geared to the passing of the civil examinations from childhood on. Hence, the importance of learning the Confucian classics. Specifically, one may ask, how could a young man or boy tackle the difficult text of the *Shi Jing*? Obviously, only with the help of some commentaries, which really meant the "Old" and the "New Commentaries." For example, it would have been crucial for an aspiring student to "know" that the song "Please, Zhongzi" was not a simple love song but a "satire" criticizing Duke Zhuang or an "licentious" song. Needless to say, these civil examinations did not encourage any original or unorthodox reading of a given text. Quite conceivably, some of these young men in their later years came to read the songs of the *Shi Jing* differently. But would they have urged their sons to follow their own reading rather than Zheng's or Zhu's?

As I close, I fear that this note might have given the reader the wrong impression that very few other commentaries have appeared since the general acceptance of Zheng's and Zhu's commentary as the standard ones. As a matter of fact, however, there appeared numerous works on the *Shi Jing*, especially during the Song and Qing periods. One of the Japanese translators I have consulted, Mekada Makoto, gives thirty titles in his list of Chinese works on the *Shi Jing*. Significantly, however, I must add, most of them are expositions of our two standard commentaries, as far as I could tell from their titles.

Notes to the Introduction

1   The title *Shi Jing* came to be used during the Han period, only after the designation of the Five Classics, which included, along with the *Shi*, the *Book of Change*, the *Book of Documents*, the *Annals of Spring–Autumn*, and the *Li* [Propriety].

2   The first song of the *Shi Jing, Guo Feng*.

3   The first two chapters of the *Shi Jing, Guo Feng*.

4   See my essay "Confucius's Aesthetic Concept of Noble Man: Beyond Moralism," in *Asian Philosophy*, Vol. 16, No. 2 (July 2006).

5   Perhaps it should be made clear that the allegorical use of a song from the *Shi Jing* in communication is one thing, and it is altogether another matter to *interpret* a given song as an allegory of a historical incident or some Confucian idea. In the latter case, one would be treating the song as a *particular* allegory as used in the past, whereas in the former case, it would be

entirely up to the user when to use the song, depending on his understanding of it *as a song* and on the given particular circumstance. In this
respect, one may say, the Confucian commentators' allegorical reading of
the *Shi Jing* was a search for *past* "allegories," whereas the allegorical use of
a song by its readers would mean its utility in *future* communication.

6 For Confucius such must be the universe of the noble man (*jun zi*), in which
both the speaker and the interlocutor can play meaningfully a
Wittgensteinian language-game. Note especially saying (7). Broadly, the
power of an allegory comes from its ability to appeal to human sentiments
directly and vividly. Hence, his saying: "By the *Shi* you may arouse people."
Again, this possibility presupposes a shared universe of humanity. For
Confucius the *Shi* helps one discover humanity's universe of sentiments.

7 I have noted the philological approach to the classics during the Qing
period, but this had much to do with textual analysis and was not to question the Confucian approach of the past.)

THE TRANSLATION

I. 周南 Zhou Nan[1]

---

[1] The heading of each chapter in "*Guo Feng*" contains the name of the region from which the songs in the chapter come. While the names of all the regions except in this and the next chapter are followed by the character *feng*, meaning each region's common custom, in these first two chapters the headings contain the character *nan* after the names of the regions, Zhou and Shao, two regions immediately south of the royal domain of the Zhou during the dynasty's earlier times: Zhou the region south of Loyang, and Shao the Xi'an and its vicinity on today's map. What does the character *nan* in these two headings, Zhou Nan and Shao Nan, mean? There are different theories regarding its meaning. The basic meaning of the character is "south." Shirakawa suggests that *nan* here connotes *music* of the south (47, 48).

1. 關雎

關關雎鳩
在河之洲
窈窕淑女
君子好逑

參差荇菜
左右流之
窈窕淑女
寤寐求之

求之不得
寤寐思服
悠哉悠哉
輾轉反側

參差荇菜
左右采之
窈窕淑女
琴瑟友之

參差荇菜
左右芼之
窈窕淑女
鍾鼓樂之

1. *Guan Guan*, Ospreys

Guan guan, cry the ospreys
On the isle of the river.
Lovely is this fine maiden,
Fit match for a nobleman.

Long and short grow water mallows,
Left and right, she seeks them.
Lovely is this fine maiden,
Day and night, you long for her.

You seek her but don't get her,
Day and night you think of her.
How sad! How sad!
Turning and tossing on your side.

Long and short grow water mallows,
Left and right, she gathers them.
Lovely is this fine maiden,
Play *qin se*,[2] let us befriend her.

Long and short grow water mallows,
Left and right, she chooses them.
Lovely is this fine maiden,
Beat *zhong gu*,[3] let us delight her.

---

[2] *Qin* and *se*, two common musical instruments, are often referred to in combination, as in this line. They look similar, but *qin* has seven strings, and *se* 25.

[3] *Zhong* and *gu*, again two common musical instruments, are also often referred to together, as in this line. Separately, *zhong* means "bell," and *gu* "drum." Note that bells in the Far East are generally to be beaten, like drums, to produce sounds.

2. 葛覃

葛之覃兮
施于中谷
維葉萋萋
黃鳥于飛
集于灌木
其鳴喈喈

葛之覃兮
施于中谷
維葉莫莫
是刈是濩
為絺為綌
服之無斁

言告師氏
言告言歸
薄污我私
薄澣我衣
害澣害否
歸寧父母

2. The Cloth-plant Spreading

How the cloth-plant spreads
Reaching the middle of the valley.
How dense its leaves.
The orioles in flight
Gather on the coppice,
Singing together *jie, jie.*

How the cloth-plant spreads
Reaching the middle of the valley.
How lush its leaves.
Pick them, steam them,
Make clothes coarse and fine.
I never tire of wearing them.

Tell my lady[4],
I am going home.
Wash my underclothes,
Wash my dress.
What to wash and what not to?
I am returning home.

---

[4] A lady who attends to a married woman to instruct her the female virtues as well as rules of propriety on various occasions.

3. 卷耳

采采卷耳
不盈頃筐
嗟我懷人
寘彼周行

陟彼崔嵬
我馬虺隤
我姑酌彼金罍
維以不永懷

陟彼高岡
我馬玄黃
我姑酌彼兕觥
維以不永傷

陟彼砠矣
我馬瘏矣
我僕痡矣
云何吁矣

3. Chickweeds[5]

I pick and pick chickweeds,
They won't fill this bamboo basket.
Ah, thinking of this man
I leave it on the road.

I climb that steep hill,
My horse is worn out.
I drink wine from that metal ewer,
To still my endless thoughts.

I climb that high hill,
My horse turns yellow.
I drink wine in a buffalo jug,
To ease my painful thoughts.

I climb that rocky hill,
My horse is exhausted.
My groom is in pain,
Oh, woe, how I mourn.

---

[5] This may be read as a song sung by a woman and her husband (or lover), who is away on the road or gone on military campaign: the first verse by the woman and the rest by the man, thinking of each other.

4. 樛木

南有樛木	4. Drooping Tree
葛藟纍之	

南有樛木
葛藟纍之
樂只君子
福履綏之

南有樛木
葛藟荒之
樂只君子
福履將之

南有樛木
葛藟縈之
樂只君子
福履成之

4. Drooping Tree

In the south grows the drooping tree,
On it, creepers thriving.[6]
Oh, happy is our lord,
Blessed, he is in peace.

In the south grows the drooping tree,
On it, creepers teeming.
Oh, happy is our lord,
Blessed, he is majestic.

In the south grows the drooping tree,
Around it, creepers spreading.
Oh, happy is our lord,
Blessed, he flourishes.

---

[6] The first two lines of each verse give an image of good fortune and abundance (Sirakawa, 62–63).

5. 螽斯

螽斯羽
詵詵兮
宜爾子孫
振振兮

螽斯羽
薨薨兮
宜爾子孫
繩繩兮

螽斯羽
揖揖兮
宜爾子孫
蟄蟄兮

5. Locusts

There fly the locusts[7]
Xian xian, in great flocks.
Truly may your offspring
Flourish in abundance.

There fly the locusts
Hong hong, in great flocks.
Truly may your offspring
Last generation after generation.

There fly the locust
Yi yi, in great flocks.
Truly may your offspring
Prosper in harmony.

---

[7] "Locusts" in flocks suggests abundance and prosperity.

6. 桃夭

桃之夭夭
灼灼其華
之子于歸
宜其室家

桃之夭夭
有蕡其實
之子于歸
宜其家室

桃之夭夭
其葉蓁蓁
之子于歸
宜其家人

6. Young Peach Tree

How youthful the peach tree,
How ablaze its flowers!
This girl is getting married,
Good for that house.[8]

How youthful the peach tree,
How ripe its fruit!
This girl is getting married,
Good for that family.

How youthful the peach tree,
How dense its leaves!
This girl is getting married,
Good for that home.

---

[8] The household the girl is married into.

7. 兔罝

肅肅兔罝
椓之丁丁
赳赳武夫
公侯干城

肅肅兔罝
施于中逵
赳赳武夫
公侯好仇

肅肅兔罝
施于中林
赳赳武夫
公侯腹心

7. Rabbit Nets

Su su, quietly they set rabbit nets,
Hammer the stakes *ting ting*.
Stout and brave are the warriors,
Shields and bulwarks of our lords.

Su su, quietly they set rabbit nets,
Spread them at the crossroads.
Stout and brave are the warriors,
Comrades of our lords.

Su su, quietly they set rabbit nets,
Spread them in the woods.
Stout and brave are the warriors,
Trusted men of our lords.

8. 芣苢

采采芣苢
薄言采之
采采芣苢
薄言有之

采采芣苢
薄言掇之
采采芣苢
薄言捋之

采采芣苢
薄言袺之
采采芣苢
薄言襭之

8. Plantain

Pluck, pluck the plantain,[9]
Pluck it.
Pluck, pluck the plantain,
You've got it.

Pluck, pluck the plantain,
Grab it.
Pluck, pluck the plantain,
You gather it.

Pluck, pluck the plantain,
Put it in the apron.
Pluck, pluck the plantain,
Collect it in your skirt.

---

[9] This plant was believed to be good for women desiring babies.

9. 漢廣

南有喬木
不可休息
漢有游女

不可求思
漢之廣矣
不可泳思
江之永矣
不可方思

翹翹錯薪
言刈其楚
之子于歸
言秣其馬
漢之廣矣
不可泳思
江之永矣
不可方思

翹翹錯薪
言刈其蔞
之子于歸
言秣其駒
漢之廣矣
不可泳思
江之永矣
不可方思

9. Broad Han[10]

In the south stands the soaring tree,
You may not rest under it.
On the Han[11] appears the goddess of the
    river,[12]
You may not lust after her.
Oh, so broad is the Han,
You may not swim it.
Oh, so long is the Jiang,[13]
You may not raft it.

Here the brushwood grows thick and tall,
I shall cut the sagebrush.
When the goddess comes to be married,
I shall feed her pony.
Oh, so broad is the Han,
You may not swim it.
Oh, so long is the Jiang,
You may not raft it.

Here the brushwood grows thick and tall,
I shall cut the brambles.
When the goddess comes to be married,
I shall feed her pony.
Oh, so broad is the Han,
You may not swim it.
Oh, so long is the Jiang,
You may not raft it.

---

[10] Yoshikawa reads this song as a song admiring the unapproachable purity of a fine maiden (Yoshikawa, 51).

[11] The Hanshui, a tributary of the Yangzi.

[12] Shirakawa's reading (71).

[13] I.e., the Yangzi.

10. 汝墳

遵彼汝墳
伐其條枚
未見君子
惄如調飢

遵彼汝墳
伐其條肆
既見君子
不我遐棄

魴魚赬尾
王室如燬
雖則如燬
父母孔邇

10. The High Banks of the Ru

Along the high banks of the Ru[14]
I go cutting boughs and stems.
Not seeing you[15]
I feel a pang like morning hunger.

Along the high banks of the Ru
I go cutting boughs and twigs.
I now see you,
You haven't deserted me.

The bream has a red tail,[16]
The royal house[17] is ablaze.
Though it is ablaze
Our parents are near us.

---

[14] A river that flows in the northwest Henan.

[15] In this line (and also in the next verse) the speaker is using the word *jun zi*, addressing her husband (see, e.g., Shirakawa, 74; Yoshikawa, 54).

[16] A fish was believed to get its tail red when strained. Reading this song (the first two verses) as a love song, Shirakawa finds the last verse probably an addition from another song (75, 76).

[17] The Shang dynasty?

11. 麟之趾

麟之趾
振振公子
于嗟麟兮

麟之定
振振公姓
于嗟麟兮

麟之角
振振公族
于嗟麟兮

11. *Qilin*'s Hoofs

The *qilin*'s hoofs,[18]
May the sons of our lord prosper.
Ah, the *qilin*!

The *qilin*'s brow,
May the offspring of our lord prosper.
Ah, the *qilin*!

The *qilin*'s horns,
May the kinsmen of our lord prosper.
Ah, the *qilin*!

---

[18] The *qilin* is an imaginary creature, an auspicious animal, whose feet never tread on growing plants or living insects. It was believed to appear in times of sage kings.

II. 召南 Shao Nan[19]

---

[19] See note 1.

12. 鵲巢

維鵲有巢
維鳩居之
之子于歸
百兩御之

維鵲有巢
維鳩方之
之子于歸
百兩將之

維鵲有巢
維鳩盈之
之子于歸
百兩成之

12. Magpie's Nest

In a magpie's nest
Lives the cuckoo.
This girl is getting married,
Welcome her with a hundred coaches.

In a magpie's nest
The cuckoo makes a home.
The girl is getting married,
Send her off with a hundred coaches.

In a magpie's nest,
The cuckoo fills it with its young.
The girl is getting married,
Celebrate it with a hundred coaches.

13. 采蘩

13. Gather the White Mugwort

于以采蘩
于沼于沚
于以用之
公侯之事

She gathers the white mugwort
By the pool, by the shallows.
Where does she use it?
At the sacrifice to the lord's ancestors.

于以采蘩
于澗之中
于以用之
公侯之宮

She gathers the white mugwort
Down in the ravine.
Where does she use it?
In the lord's ancestral hall.

被之僮僮
夙夜在公
被之祁祁
薄言還歸

Her wig, tall and solemn,
She attends the sacrifice through the night.
Her wig, moving quietly,
She withdraws to her room.

14. 草蟲

喓喓草蟲
趯趯阜螽
未見君子
憂心忡忡
亦既見止
亦既覯止
我心則降。

陟彼南山
言采其蕨
未見君子
憂心惙惙
亦既見止
亦既覯止
我心則說

陟彼南山
言采其薇
未見君子
我心傷悲
亦既見止
亦既覯止
我心則夷

14. Cicada

The cicada chirps,
The grasshopper skips.
Not seeing you,
My heart was anxious.
I see you,
Now we are together,
My heart is calm.

I climbed the south hill,
Gathered the bracken.
Not seeing you,
My heart fretted.
I see you,
Now we are together,
My heart is joyful.

I climbed the south hill,
Gathered the bracken.
Not seeing you,
My heart was in pain.
I see you,
Now we are together,
My heart is at rest.

15. 采蘋

于以采蘋
南澗之濱
于以采藻
于彼行潦

于以盛之
維筐及筥
于以湘之
維錡及釜

于以奠之
宗室牖下
誰起尸之
有齊季女。

15. Gather the Duckweed

Gather the duckweed
By the banks of the south stream.
We gather water-grass
In that little creek.

Put them
In bamboo baskets, round and square.
Boil them
In pots and kettles.

Place them
Under the door of the ancestral hall.
Who offers them at the sacrifice?
The youngest maiden, the pure one.

16. 甘棠

蔽芾甘棠
勿翦勿伐
召伯所茇

蔽芾甘棠
勿翦勿敗
召伯所憩

蔽芾甘棠
勿翦勿拜
召伯所說

16. Wild Pear Tree[20]

How thriving is this wild pear tree!
Do not lop or cut it,
The Lord of Shao camped under it.

How thriving is this wild pear tree!
Do not lop or harm it,
The Lord of Shao rested under it.

How thriving is this wild pear tree!
Do not lop or uproot it,
The Lord of Shao slept under it.

---

[20] According to tradition, this poem was sung by the people of Shao in praise of the benevolent rule of the Lord of Shao. He was believed to have stayed under this wild pear tree during his visit to this village, instead of troubling the villagers for his sojourn.

17. 行露

厭浥行露
豈不夙夜
謂行多露

誰謂雀無角
何以穿我屋
誰謂女無家
何以速我獄

雖速我獄
室家不足

誰謂鼠無牙
何以穿我墉
誰謂女無家
何以速我訟

雖速我獄
亦不女從

17. Dew-Drenched Path

The path was drenched with dew,
Wasn't it late at night?
I said too much dew on the path.

Who says the sparrow has no beak?
How come it bores a hole in my roof?
Who says you have no family?
How come this suit is brought
    against me?[21]
Though you bring this suit against me,
This will not bring us together.

Who says the rat has no teeth?
How come it bores a hole in my wall?
Who says you have no family?
How come this plaint is brought
    against me?
Though you bring this plaint against me,
Still I will not marry you.

---

[21] Apparently in ancient times, a young woman could be brought before the magistrate for rejecting a proper marriage arrangement.

18. 羔羊

羔羊之皮
素絲五紽
退食自公
委蛇委蛇

羔羊之革
素絲五緎
委蛇委蛇
自公退食

羔羊之縫
素絲五總
委蛇委蛇
退食自公

18. Lamb Skins

In lamb skins
Sewn with white silk thread in five strands,
He is withdrawing from office for meal,
In easy, staid steps.

In lamb hides
Sewn with white silk thread in five strands,
In easy, staid steps,
He is withdrawing from office for meal.

In a lamb skin coat
Sewn with white silk thread in five strands,
In with easy, staid steps,
He is withdrawing from office for meal.

19. 殷其靁

殷其靁
在南山之陽
何斯違斯
莫敢或遑
振振君子
歸哉歸哉

殷其靁
在南山之側
何斯違斯
莫敢遑息
振振君子
歸哉歸哉

殷其靁
在南山之下
何斯違斯
莫敢遑處
振振君子
歸哉歸哉

19. The Thunder Rolling

The thunder rolling
On the sunny side of the south hill,
Why must you be on the road again?
Never seeking to take rest?
My tender husband,
Come back to me, come back to me.

The thunder rolling
Along the south hill,
Why must you be on the road again?
Never seeking to take leave?
My tender husband,
Come back to me, come back to me.

The thunder rolling
Below the south hill.
Why must you be on the road again?
Never seeking to take rest?
My tender husband,
Come back to me, come back to me.

20. 摽有梅

摽有梅
其實七兮
求我庶士
迨其吉兮

摽有梅
其實三兮
求我庶士
迨其今兮

摽有梅
頃筐墍之
求我庶士
迨其謂之

20. Plum Throwing

I am throwing the plums,[22]
Ah, seven of them left.[23]
Any man desiring me,
This is your fine chance.

I am throwing the plums,
Ah, three of them left.
Any man desiring me,
Now is your chance.

I am throwing the plums,
Ah, the bamboo basket is empty.
Any man desiring me,
It's time to say so.

---

[22] There are several different readings of this song. This translation follows Shirakawa (100–102) and Mekada (17–18). According to the custom of the time, young women would throw plums or other fruits at men they liked. See No. 64, "Quince."

[23] This line in the Chinese text simply says "Ah, seven of them." In view of the other two verses, one may read it as "seven of them remaining."

21. 小星

嘒彼小星
三五在東
肅肅宵征
夙夜在公
寔命不同。

嘒彼小星
維參與昴
肅肅宵征
抱衾與裯
寔命不猶

21. Little Stars[24]

Those little stars twinkling,
Three or five in the east.
In silence, we walk through the dark,
It's still night in the palace.
Truly fates are not equal.

Those little stars twinkling,
Orion and the Pleiades.
In silence, we walk through the dark,
Carrying coverlets and bedclothes.
Truly fates are not the same.

---

[24] This song is commonly read as the song of a court lady lamenting her fate compared with that of the wife of her lord or of someone favored by him.

22. 江有汜

22. The Yangzi Has its Branches

江有汜
之子歸
不我以
不我以
其後也悔

The Yangzi has its branches.
This lady goes to be married
Without taking us along.[25]
Without taking us along,
She will be sorry later.

江有渚
之子歸
不我與
不我與
其後也處

The Yangzi has its islands.
This lady goes to be married
Without taking us with her.
Without taking us with her,
She will grieve later.

江有沱
之子歸
不我過
不我過
其嘯也歌

The Yangzi has its forks.
This lady goes to be married
Without stopping to see us.
Without stopping to see us,
She will sing a lament later.

---

[25] When a lady was to get married in old times, it was customary to take her bridesmaids along with her. This song is variously read. The *Yangzi*, of course, has many branches and islands. This lady, who goes to get married "without taking us along", is compared to a large river without its branches.

23. 野有死麕

23. Dead Roe Deer in the Field

野有死麕	A roe deer lies dead in the field.[26]
白茅包之	Wrap it in white rushes.[27]
有女懷春	A girl dreams of spring,[28]
吉士誘之	A monk[29] seduces her.
林有樸樕	Brushes grow in the wood,
野有死鹿	A deer lies dead in the field.[30]
白茅純束	Bundle it in white rushes,
有女如玉	There is a girl as fair as jade.
舒而脫脫兮	Ah, don't rush, slowly, slowly.
無感我帨兮	Don't touch the towel on my girdle,
無使尨也吠	Don't let the dog bark.

---

[26] In this opening line, the character *jin* refers to a small species of roe deer (*hydropotes inermis argyropus*), which grows no antler.

[27] To give it as a present to a girl.

[28] Meaning a girl who is eager to have a man.

[29] Shirakawa's reading (107).

[30] In this line the character *lu* is used to mean the common species of deer, in contrast with *jin* earlier. Generally, the difference between *lu* and *jin* is ignored by commentators. But it seems that the key to the understanding of this song lies in the recognition of the difference. Takata notes that sending a *jin* is a cheaper act of gift than sending a *lu*, though he does not pursue this implication (see Takata, 93). The song seems to suggest that a *jin* is a gift for a girl who deserves a seducer, whereas a *lu* is a gift for a girl who is as pure or fair "as jade."

24. 何彼襛矣

24. How Resplendent

何彼襛矣	How resplendent
唐棣之華	Are those blossoms of the cherry!
曷不肅雝	How dignified and lovely
王姬之車	Are those carriages of the royal bride!
何彼襛矣	How resplendent
華如桃李	Are those blossoms, like peach and apricot flowers!
平王之孫	She is granddaughter of King Ping,[31]
齊侯之子	Child of the Duke of Qi.
其釣維何	What do you angle fish with?[32]
維絲伊緡	A line twined with silk thread.
齊侯之子	She is child of the Duke of Qi,
平王之孫	Granddaughter of King Ping.

---

[31] The thirteenth king of the Zhou dynasty (770–719 BCE).

[32] The image of angling fish is often used in songs of marriage

25. 騶虞

25. *Zouyu*[33]

彼茁者葭
壹發五犯
于嗟乎騶虞

There thrive the reeds in the field.
At one shot five boars.
Ah, the marvelous *zouyu*.[34]

彼茁者蓬
壹發五豵
于嗟乎騶虞

There thrives the sagebrush in the field.
At one shot five yearlings.
Ah, the marvelous *zouyu*.

---

[33] An auspicious mythological animal, which was believed to appear during the rule of a sage king, a creature which looks like a white tiger with patterns in black, and does not eat living beings.

[34] There are different readings of *zouyu* in this line. According to one view, *zouyu* designated officials of the royal hunting grounds. I follow this reading (see Takata, 99).

III. 邶風　Bei Feng[35]

---

[35] The three chapters beginning with "Bei Feng" contain songs from the state of Wei, situated in the northern part of today's Henan. "Bei" in the title of this chapter, as "Yong" in that of the next, was originally the name of a separate state, but later became a part of Wei.

26. 柏舟

汎彼柏舟
亦汎其流
耿耿不寐
如有隱憂
微我無酒
以敖以遊

我心匪鑒
不可以茹
亦有兄弟
不可以據
薄言往愬
逢彼之怒。

我心匪石
不可轉也
我心匪席
不可卷也
威儀棣棣
不可選也

憂心悄悄
慍于群小
覯閔既多
受侮不少
靜言思之
寤辟有摽

日居月諸
胡迭而微
心之憂矣
如匪澣衣
靜言思之
不能奮飛

26. Cypress Boat[36]

Adrift, that cypress boat
Flows down the river.
Dan dan I am sleepless,
As though in deep anguish.
Wine I do have,
It may cheer me up.

My heart is not a mirror,
It cannot reflect.
Brothers too I have,
They are not to be counted on.
Once I went to them for help,
I met their anger.

My heart is not a stone,
It cannot be turned over.
My heart is not a mat,
It cannot be rolled away.
My conduct blameless,
None can pick my failures.

Unbearable is my grieving heart,
I resent those mean-spirited ones.
I have suffered malice plenty,
Received insults not few.
In silence, thinking of this,
I stay awake, my heart pounding.

Oh, sun and moon,
Why do you eclipse each other?
My heart in sorrow
Is like unwashed clothes.
In silence, thinking of this,
I wish I could fly away.

27. 綠衣

綠兮衣兮
綠兮黃裏
心之憂矣
曷維其已

綠兮衣兮
綠兮黃裳
心之憂矣
曷維其亡

綠兮絲兮
女所治兮
我思古人
俾無訧兮

絺兮綌兮
淒其以風
我思古人
實獲我心。

27. Green Dress[37]

Ah, the green dress,
The green dress, the yellow lining.
My heart is grieving,
Will this ever end?

Ah, the green dress,
The green dress, the yellow skirt.
My heart is grieving,
Will this ever cease?

Ah, the green thread,
You spun it.
I think of you, now gone,
You lived blameless.

Ah, this thin hemp shirt,
The cold wind is blowing.
I think of you, now gone,
Truly you captured my heart.

---

[36] Shirakawa reads this song as a lamentation of a woman who has suffered much misfortune, possibly unhappy marriage (120). The song doesn't give any indication of the source of her anxiety or misery. However, it may not be hard to imagine many possible sources of misfortune, especially for women in the patriarchal Zhou society.

[37] Many commentators read this song, interpreting the meaning of the phrase "green dress" in terms of Confucian symbolism. Rejecting such a reading, Shirakawa reads it simply as a song in which the grieving husband thinks of his deceased wife, looking at her old green dress (122, 123). See also Shirakawa's work *Shikyō*, p. 37, for her criticism of the Confucian reading of the song. I essentially follow her reading, which seems only natural. One wonders if the Confucian commentators of the past were unable or unwilling to allow the surviving husband's grieving as something a true gentlemen might do.

28. 燕燕

燕燕于飛
差池其羽
之子于歸
遠送于野
瞻望弗及
泣涕如雨

燕燕于飛
頡之頏之
之子于歸
遠于將之
瞻望弗及
佇立以泣

燕燕于飛
下上其音
之子于歸
遠送于南
瞻望弗及
實勞我心

仲氏任只
其心塞淵
終溫且惠
淑慎其身
先君之思
以勗寡人

28. Swallows, Swallows[38]

Swallows, swallows in flight,
Flapping their wings.
She is returning home,
I send her off in the field.
She is far now, out of sight,
Tears flow like rain.

Swallows, swallows in flight,
Now up, now down.
She is returning home,
Far, far I escort her.
She is far now, out of sight,
Standing still, I weep.

Swallows, swallows in flight,
Up and down, calling.
She is returning home.
I send her off to the south.
She is far now, out of sight,
Truly my heart is saddened.

How considerate she was,
Her heart true, never frivolous.
Always gentle and loving,
Her bearing graceful and courteous.
Mindful of our late lord,
She encouraged me.

---

[38] Traditionally, this poem is read as a song in which Zhuang Jiang, the wife of Duke Zhuang, sends off one of his secondary wives, after the death of the Duke. This reading may make sense especially in view of the final verse (the last two lines). However, this last verse appears, in more than one way, out of line with the preceding ones, which one may read *simply* as a song in which one lady is sending off another (Yoshikawa, 109). The final verse may be a later addition.

29. 日月

日居月諸
照臨下土
乃如之人兮
逝不古處
胡能有定
寧不我顧

日居月諸
下土是冒
乃如之人兮
逝不相好
胡能有定
寧不我報

日居月諸
出自東方
乃如之人兮
德音無良
胡能有定
俾也可忘

日居月諸
東方自出
父兮母兮
畜我不卒
胡能有定
報我不述

29. Sun and Moon[39]

Oh, sun, oh, moon,
Shine on the earth below.
A man like this
Never settles down in life.
How can he be relied upon?
He no longer turns to me.

Oh, sun, oh, moon,
Cover the earth below.
A man like this
Is never kind to others.
How can he be relied upon?
He no longer responds to me.

Oh, sun, oh, moon,
Rise from the east.
A man like this
Never says fine words.
How can he be relied upon?
I wish I could forget him.

Oh, sun, oh, moon,
From the east they rise.
Oh, father, oh, mother,
You have raised me to no good end.
How can he be relied upon?
He doesn't treat me right.

---

[39] A wife's song lamenting her faithless husband.

30. 終風

終風且暴
顧我則笑
謔浪笑敖
中心是悼

終風且霾
惠然肯來
莫往莫來
悠悠我思

終風且曀
不日有曀
寤言不寐
願言則嚔

曀曀其陰
虺虺其靁
寤言不寐
願言則懷

30. Windy Day

That windy day was so violent,
You looked at me and laughed.
Joking wildly, sneering cruelly,
My heart was in pain.

That windy day so stormy,
Kindly you agreed to come.
You neither went nor came.
Endless were my thoughts.

That windy day so dark,
So dark without sun.
Awake, my sleep is gone,
Deep in thought, I sigh.

How dark the clouds,
Thunder growling,
Awake, sleep is gone,
Deep in thought, my heart cries.

31. 擊鼓

擊鼓其鏜
踊躍用兵
土國城漕

我獨南行

從孫子仲
平陳與宋
不我以歸
憂心有忡

爰居爰處
爰喪其馬
于以求之
于林之下

死生契闊
與子成說
執子之手
與子偕老

于嗟闊兮
不我活兮
于嗟洵兮
不我信兮

31. Beat the Drums

Tang tang, the drums beating,
They leap swinging their weapons,
They build walls in the capital, fortifying
    Cao.[40]
We alone march to the south.

Led by Sun Zizhong,
We came to subdue Chen and Song,
But now we are left behind.
My mind is full of worries.

Here we stay, here we camp,
Here we lose a horse,
We search for it
In the woods.

With you I swore
To live and die through hardship,
Holding your hands,
I vowed to grow old together.

Ah, so far away!
I no longer live with you.
Ah, so far away!
I no longer keep my words to you.

---

[40] A town in the state of Wei.

45

32. 凱風

凱風自南
吹彼棘心
棘心夭夭
母氏劬勞

凱風自南
吹彼棘薪
母氏聖善
我無令人

爰有寒泉
在浚之下
有子七人
母氏勞苦

睍睆黃鳥
載好其音
有子其人
莫慰母心

32. Gentle Breeze[41]

A gentle breeze from the south
Blows to the budding thorn-bushes.
Young and tender are the buds,
Our caring mother toils day and night.

A gentle breeze from the south
Blows to the hard thorn-bushes.
Our mother is wise and kind,
None among us is a decent man.

There is a cold spring
Outside the town of Jun.
She has seven sons,
She toils day and night.

Bright orioles,
How pleasant are their songs!
She has seven sons,
None comforts the mother's heart.

---

[41] As some commentators suggest, this poem seems based on the story of a woman who worked hard to raise seven sons, none of whom, however, grew up to relieve her of her hardship. See Shirakawa, 137 and Waley, 71. Is one of her sons lamenting his mother's life of hardship in this poem?

33. 雄雉

雄雉于飛
泄泄其羽
我之懷矣
自詒伊阻

雄雉于飛
下上其音
展矣君子
實勞我心

瞻彼日月
悠悠我思
道之云遠
曷云能來

百爾君子
不知德行
不忮不求
何用不臧

33. Cock-pheasant

The cock-pheasant flies up,
Flapping its wings.
It is my love for you
That has brought me this trouble.

The cock-pheasant flies up.
Crying high and low.
Truly it's you
That wears out my heart.

I look up at the sun, the moon,
Endless are my thoughts.
The road to you is so far,
When will you come home?

Oh, gentlemen,
You don't know what true virtue is.
I hurt none, I seek nothing,
Wouldn't this be good enough?

34. 匏有苦葉　　34. The Gourd Has Bitter Leaves

匏有苦葉　　　　The gourd has bitter leaves,
濟有深涉　　　　The ford is deep to cross.
深則厲　　　　　If it's deep, take off your clothes,
淺則揭　　　　　If it's shallow, tuck up your skirts.

有瀰濟盈　　　　The ford is in full flood,
有鷕雉鳴　　　　Wistful is the pheasant's call.
濟盈不濡軌　　　So why not let the axle get wet?[42]
雉鳴求其牡　　　The pheasant is seeking her mate.

雝雝鳴鴈　　　　In unison the geese are crying,
旭日始旦　　　　Sunrise, it's daybreak.
士如歸妻　　　　Young man, if you seek your bride,
迨冰未泮　　　　Cross the ice before it breaks away.

招招舟子　　　　The boatman beckons, calling.
人涉卬否　　　　Others may cross, not I,
人涉卬否　　　　Others may cross, not I.
卬須我友　　　　I will wait for my girl.

---

[42] This line (*ji ying bu ru gui*) is usually translated: "The ford is deep, yet the axle does not get wet." But see Takata, 145.

35. 谷風

習習谷風
以陰以雨
黽勉同心
不宜有怒
采葑采菲
無以下體
德音莫違
及爾同死

行道遲遲
中心有違
不遠伊邇
薄送我畿
誰謂荼苦
其甘如薺
宴爾新昏
如兄如弟

涇以渭濁
湜湜其沚
宴爾新昏
不我屑以
毋逝我梁
毋發我笱
我躬不閱
遑恤我後

35. Valley Wind

Xi xi, blows the valley wind,
Bringing clouds, bringing rain.
"Strive to be of one mind,
Never be angry with each other."
"You pick turnips and radishes,
Not by the lowers parts."[43]
Never lose your kind voice,
And I will be with you till death.

I was leaving home, walking slowly,
Heavy in heart.
You didn't accompany me far,
Sent me off at the gate.
Who says the sow thistle is bitter?
It's as sweet as the shepherd's purse.
You enjoy your new bride,
As though your own sister.

It's the Wei that makes the Jing dirty.[44]
How clear its shoals!
You enjoy your new bride,
And see me not good enough for you.
Don't go near my fish-dam,
Don't touch my fish-traps.
I have been abandoned,
Why should I care about what's left
    behind me?

---

[43] Though one usually eats only the lower parts. Probably cited in these four lines in the middle of this verse are two common sayings.

[44] The Jing, a river in Shaanxi, later flows into the Wei.

42

就其深矣　　　Coming to deep water,
方之舟之　　　I rafted it, boated it.
就其淺矣　　　Coming to shallow water,
泳之游之　　　I swam over and under it.
何有何亡　　　Whatever was available or not,
黽勉求之　　　I strove to find it.
凡民有喪　　　When the neighbors were in trouble,
匍匐救之　　　I did my utmost to help them.

不我能慉　　　Instead of caring for me,
反以我為讎　　You regard me as your enemy.
既阻我德　　　You dim my good reputation,
賈用不售　　　This ware will not sell.
昔育恐育鞫　　In the past, to relieve this family of
　　　　　　　　　poverty,
及爾顛覆　　　With you I toiled like a slave.
既生既育　　　Now that the family is well-off,
比予于毒　　　You treat me as if I am poison.

我有旨蓄　　　I have kept a good store of food,
亦以御冬　　　So you will again make it through this
　　　　　　　　　winter.

宴爾新昏　　　Enjoy your new bride,
以我御窮　　　You will survive, thanks to me.
有洸有潰　　　Your violence, your abuse,
既詒我肄　　　You gave me so much hardship.
不念昔者　　　Don't you remember those early days,
伊余來墍　　　When I came and we lived happily?

36. 式微

式微　式微
胡不歸
微君之故
胡為乎中露

式微　式微
胡不歸
微君之躬
胡為乎泥中

36. How Wretched[45]

How wretched, how wretched!
Why not return?
Were it not for your sake,
What should I be doing here in the dew?

How wretched, how wretched!
Why not return?
Were it not for you,
What should I be doing here in the mud?

---

[45] Traditionally, this song is interpreted in view of some historical incident or other. Shirakawa, however, reads it as a song in which a woman is urging her man to give up whatever detains him in the present wretched condition, and to return to their old village (149).

37. 旄丘

旄丘之葛兮
何誕之節兮
叔兮伯兮
何多日也

何其處也
必有與也
何其久也
必有以也

狐裘蒙戎
匪車不東

叔兮伯兮
靡所與同

37. Scrubby Hill

The cloth-plant on the scrubby hill,
How far apart its joints have grown!
Uncles, elders,[46]
Why so many days?

What makes you stay there?
You must have company with you.
Why so long?
You must have reason.

My fox fur coat is tattered and frayed.
There is no wagon that hasn't gone to
　　the east.
Uncles, elders,
You no longer share life with us.

---

[46] Who are these "uncles" and "elders"? Are they soldiers gone on a military campaign? The poem has been read in various ways. I read it as a poem in which the wives left behind are wondering or rather questioning why their husbands were so long gone, not necessarily distrusting them. Let us keep in mind that they were living in the ancient world, in which few of the common populace would have known such things as public information or letter-writing, and were utterly in the dark, except through rumors, as to why their "uncles and elders" were gone away for so long, and who were or what was keeping them, and where, once these men were taken away from them. Indeed, people would have had little conception of war, engaged by the ruler or government, which might have appeared to them like some invisible, mysterious agent wielding power of coercion. Or else, for them going to war was merely what men folks were expected to join, just as going away to work at a far-away place building levees along the flooded Yellow River—except that in a war they were going to participate in a mass killing for an unknown length, and nobody knew when and whether they would ever return home.

52

瑣兮尾兮　　How wretched and fallen you are!
流離之子　　You, stragglers!
叔兮伯兮　　Uncles, elders,
褎如充耳　　How flashy you are, with your ear-plugs![47]

---

[47] Ear ornaments.

38. 簡兮

38. How Stately

簡兮簡兮
方將萬舞
日之方中
在前上處

How stately, how stately,
He is about to do the Wan dance.[48]
The sun high in the middle of the sky,
He is up on the stage, in the front row.

碩人俁俁
公庭萬舞

How mighty this tall man looks!
He is dancing the Wan dance in the duke's
    yard!

有力如虎
執轡如組

Strong as a tiger,
He holds the reins as though ribbons.

左手執籥
右手秉翟
赫如渥赭
公言錫爵

The flute in the left hand,
The pheasant plume in the right,
His face red as though smeared with ochre.
The duke hands him a goblet.

山有榛
隰有苓
云誰之思
西方美人
彼美人兮
西方之人兮

On the hill grows the hazel tree,
On the lowland the licorice.
Of whom is he thinking?
Of the noble man of the west.
Ah, the noble man
Of the west![49]

---

[48] A group dance by men.

[49] Why suddenly this last verse, referring to the "noble man of the west" in the dancer's mind? Traditionally, this poem is to be understood especially in view of these last lines, which have nothing to do with the dance. Indeed, the poem reads like one about the dancer as person ("big man"), and less about his dancing manner. Words such as "stately," "strong," "grand manner" may be read more properly as describing the man rather than his dancing manner. I follow the usual reading of "the noble man of the west" as the Zhou king, under whose wise rule every man of talent would find his rightful place. The dancer in this poem is a "big man," which means man of extraordinary quality or capacity, but he is merely a dancer at this court of the duke of Wei. Hence his longing for the "noble man of the west."

39. 泉水　　　39. Spring Water

毖彼泉水　　　That spring water gushing out
亦流于淇　　　Flows into the Qi.[50]
有懷于衛　　　How I long for Wei!
靡日不思　　　No day passes without that thought.
孌彼諸姬　　　How dear are my cousins!
聊與之謀　　　I take counsel with them.[51]

出宿于泲　　　"On my journey leaving Wei, I lodged at Zi,
飲餞于禰　　　Drank my farewell wine at Ni.
女子有行　　　A girl going away to be married
遠父母兄弟　　Leaves behind her parents and brothers.
問我諸姑　　　I shall visit all my aunts,
遂及伯姊　　　Also my eldest sister."

出宿于干　　　"On your journey to Wei,[52] you should lodge at
　　　　　　　　　Gan,
飲餞于言　　　Drink your farewell wine at Yan.
載脂載舝　　　Oil the wheels, tighten the axle,
還車言邁　　　Before resuming your ride.
遄臻于衛　　　You will soon reach Wei,
不瑕有害　　　What mishap would happen to you?"

---

[50] One of the main rivers in Wei.

[51] This is a poem of a woman longing to visit her parents in Wei. Its mentioning of several particular place names seem to indicate that it is based on an actual story.

[52] For the reading of *chu* in this line and also in the previous one, I follow Yoshikawa (152, 153).

我思肥泉	I think of Fei Quan,[53]
茲之永歎	With a long sigh,
思須與漕	I think of Xu and Cao,[54]
我心悠悠	My heart pounding.
駕言出游	Get the carriage ready for a ride,
以寫我憂	That I may be rid of this grief.

---

[53] The name of a river.

[54] Both the names of places in Wei. The poem doesn't indicate why the woman thinks of these places. One may only assume that there are untold episodes in the actual story on which the poem is based, probably a story with which people of Wei then were familiar.

40. 北門

出自北門
憂心殷殷
終窶且貧
莫知我艱
已焉哉
天實為之
謂之何哉

王事適我
政事一埤益我
我入自外
室人交徧讁我
已焉哉
天實為之
謂之何哉

王事敦我
政事一埤遺我
我入自外
室人交徧摧我
已焉哉
天實為之
謂之何哉

40. North Gate

I go out the north gate,
Deep in my despair,
Utterly destitute, impoverished.
Nobody knows my misfortune.
All is over.
Truly, it's Heaven's doing,
Why speak of it?

The king's business comes to me,
Government business is piled on me.
I come home from work,
Everybody in the house blames me.
All is over.
Truly, it's Heaven's doing,
Why speak of it?

The king's business is sent down to me,
Government business keeps piling on me.
I come home from work,
Everybody in the house reproaches me.
All is over.
Truly, it's Heaven's doing,
Why speak of it?

41. 北風　　　41. North Wind

北風其涼　　Cold blows the north wind,
雨雪其雱　　Heavy falls the snow.
惠而好我　　If you really love me,
攜手同行　　Take my hand and go with me.
其虛其邪　　Don't waver, don't tarry.
既亟只且　　Quick!

北風其喈　　The north wind whistles,
雨雪其霏　　The falling snow blinding.
惠而好我　　If you really love me,
攜手同歸　　Take my hand and go with me.
其虛其邪　　Don't waver, don't tarry.
既亟只且　　Quick!

莫赤匪狐　　Nothing is red unless it's a fox,
莫黑匪烏　　Nothing is black unless it's a crow.[55]
惠而好我　　If you really love me,
攜手同車　　Take my hand and ride with me.
其虛其邪　　Don't waver, don't tarry.
既亟只且　　Quick!

---

[55] Both fox and crow are considered animals of bad omen.

42. 靜女　　　42. Quiet Girl

靜女其姝　　　Quiet girl, so pretty,
俟我於城隅　　She was to wait for me at the corner of the wall.[56]
愛而不見　　　Hiding,[57] she didn't appear,
搔首踟躕　　　Scratching my head, I paced back and forth.

靜女其孌　　　Quiet girl, so lovely,
貽我彤管　　　She gave me a red flute,
彤管有煒　　　Deep crimson.
說懌女美　　　How delightful is her beauty!

自牧歸荑　　　Coming from the meadow, she gives me
　　　　　　　　　reed-ears.
洵美且異　　　Truly beautiful and special.
匪女以為美　　I don't mean you[58] are beautiful,
美人之貽　　　You are a gift from a beautiful woman.

---

[56] Of the city wall.
[57] Tentative. The character *ai* is read in many different ways (see Takata, 179).
[58] Addressing the reed-ears. See Takata, 180.

43. 新臺

新臺有泚
河水瀰瀰
燕婉之求
籧篨不鮮

新臺有洒
河水浼浼
燕婉之求
籧篨不殄

魚網之設
鴻則離之
燕婉之求
得此戚施

43. New Terrace[59]

Bright shines the new terrace,
Boundless spreads the Huang He.[60]
He has come seeking a lovely mate,
Finds a pigeon-breasted woman barely alive.

High rises the new terrace,
The river washes over the shore.
He has come seeking a lovely mate,
Finds a pigeon-breasted woman not quite dead.

You spread fish nets
But catch a wild goose tangled.
He has come seeking a lovely mate,
Gets a cripple.

---

[59] The following poem is commonly read as a satire criticizing the extreme debauchery of Duke Xuan of Wei. According to the *Zuo Chuan*, a woman was being brought from Qi to marry the duke's son, Ji. Duke Xuan, finding her beautiful, decided to take her as his own wife. Apparently, the duke had had this "new terrace" built for his son to receive his bride. The story in the poem does not agree with the episode, but it was meant to be a satire; probably people of Wei, familiar with the incident, understood its hidden meaning.

[60] The Yellow River.

44. 二子乘舟

44. Two of You in a Boat[61]

二子乘舟　　　　Two of you riding in a boat,
汎汎其景　　　　Your figures drifting, drifting away.
願言思子　　　　Anxiously I think of you,
中心養養　　　　My heart pounding.

二子乘舟　　　　Two of you riding in a boat,
汎汎其逝　　　　Floating, floating away.
願言思子　　　　Anxiously I think of you,
不瑕有害　　　　May no calamity befall you.

---

[61] This poem too is traditionally read in light of a tragic incident involving Ji, the son of Duke Xuan of Wei. In this incident, Ji and his step-brother, Shou, are assassinated on their way to Qi, due to an intrigue plotted by another step-brother of Shuo's. One commentator speculates that this poem was sung by Shou's wet-nurse. According to the *Zuo Chuan*, Ji and Shou left for Qi separately. Hence, "two of you leaving in a boat" may be read simply as an image for their shared end.

IV. 鄘風　Yong Feng[62]

---

[62] For this chapter title, see note 35.

45. 柏舟

汎彼柏舟
在彼中河
髧彼兩髦
實維我儀
之死矢靡它
母也天只
不諒人只

汎彼柏舟
在彼河側
髧彼兩髦
實維我特
之死矢靡慝
母也天只
不諒人只

45. Cypress Boat

Afloat is that cypress boat
In the middle of the river.
That man, two hanging locks over his brow,
Will truly be my mate.
Till death I vow no one else will be.
Oh Mother, oh Heaven,
You don't understand my heart.

Afloat is that cypress boat
Near the river bank.
That man, two hanging locks over his brow,
Will truly be my companion for life.
Till death I vow no one else will be.
Oh Mother, oh Heaven,
You don't understand my heart.

46. 牆有茨

46. Star-thistle Over the Wall

牆有茨
不可埽也
中冓之言
不可道也
所可道也
言之醜也

Star-thistle grows over the wall,
Don't clear it away.
What is said in the bed-chamber
May not be told,
When told,
It would be an ugly story.

牆有茨
不可襄也
中冓之言
不可詳也
所可詳也
言之長也

Star-thistle grows over the wall,
Don't pull it away.
What is said in the bed-chamber
May not be revealed in full,
When revealed,
It would be a long story.

牆有茨
不可束也
中冓之言
不可讀也
所可讀也
言之辱也。

Star-thistle grows over the wall,
Don't remove it.
What is said in the bed-chamber
May not be recited,
When recited,
It would be a shameful story.[63]

---

[63] Traditionally this song is read as a ballad referring to the corrupt, wanton life inside the palace walls of the court of Wei. After the death of Duke Xuan, his son Shuo, who had plotted with his mother the assassination of his two older brothers, succeeds him. His mother, that is, Duke Xuan's widow, then makes love with her own step-son, Wan, born from another woman. The widow was the very woman whom Duke Xuan had snatched from his son, Ji, as she had been brought from the neighboring state, Qi, to marry the young man. (See note 59).

47. 君子偕老

君子偕老
副笄六珈
委佗委佗
如山如河
象服是宜

子之不淑
云如之何

玼兮玼兮
其之翟也
鬒髪如雲
不屑髢也
玉之瑱也
象之揥也
揚且之皙也
胡然而天也
胡然而帝也

瑳兮瑳兮
其之展也
蒙彼縐絺
是紲袢也
子之清揚
揚且之顔也
展如之人兮
邦之媛也

47. Companion Till Death

Your companion till death.[64]
From her hairpins hang six gems,
Ah, stately, gracious,
Like mountain, like river.
How well her embroidered gown
   suits her.

That she should suffer misfortune,[65]
How was it possible?

How resplendent, how resplendent
Her pheasant-wing dress.
Her black hair like clouds,
She shuns false side-locks.
Ear-plugs of jade,
A small ivory comb in her hair,
Her brow high and white.
Oh, as though she were from Heaven,
As though she were a goddess.

How gorgeous, how gorgeous
Her red silk robe.
Underneath it white crêpe,
Her thin undergarments.
Her eyebrows clear,
Her forehead high.
Truly such a lady
Is the beauty of the land!

---

[64] This line expresses the vow of marriage. It is commonly taken to refer to the marriage of Lady Xuan of Wei.

[65] Shirakawa's reading (178–9). (See also Mekada, 40).The phrase *bu shu* in this line is commonly read in the sense of immoral or indecent, as the poem is traditionally interpreted to refer to the debauchery of the wife of Duke Xuan of Wei.

48. 桑中

爱采唐矣
沬之鄉矣
云誰之思
美孟姜矣
期我乎桑中
要我乎上宫
送我乎淇之上矣

爱采麥矣
沬之北矣
云誰之思
美孟弋矣
期我乎桑中
要我乎上宫
送我乎淇之上矣

爱采葑矣
沬之東矣
云誰之思
美孟庸矣
期我乎桑中
要我乎上宫
送我乎淇之上矣

48. Mulberry Field[66]

Let's gather the dodder
In the village of Mo.
Whom am I thinking of?
The lovely Jiang sister.
She waits for me in the mulberry field,
Meets me at Shang Gong,
Accompanies me to the banks of the Qi.

Let's reap the wheat
North of Mo.
Whom am I thinking of?
The lovely Yi sister.
She waits for me in the mulberry field,
Meets me at Shang Gong,
Accompanies me to the banks of the Qi.

Let's gather the charlock
East of Mo.
Whom am I thinking of?
The lovely Yong sister.
She waits for me in the mulberry field,
Meets me at Shang Gong,
Accompanies me to the banks of the Qi.

---

[66] Shirakawa reads this song as a song sung by mulberry-picking girls (182).

49. 鶉之奔奔

49. How Quarrelsome the Quails

鶉之奔奔
鵲之彊彊
人之無良
我以為兄

How quarrelsome the quails!
How rapacious the magpies!
How mean this man!
I am to call him "brother"!

鵲之彊彊
鶉之奔奔
人之無良
我以為君

How rapacious the magpies!
How quarrelsome the quails!
How mean this man!
I am to call him "lord"!

50. 定之方中

定之方中
作于楚宮
揆之以日
作于楚室
樹之榛栗
椅桐梓漆
爰伐琴瑟

升彼虛矣
以望楚矣
望楚與堂
景山與京
降觀于桑
卜云其吉
終然允臧

靈雨既零
命彼倌人
星言夙駕
說于桑田
匪直也人
秉心塞淵
騋牝三千

50. Pegasus in the Middle of the Sky[67]

Pegasus in the middle of the southern sky,
We are building the palace on the Chu hill.
Setting the direction by the sun,
We are building the Chu palace.
We will plant hazels, chestnuts,
Catalpas, paulownias, lacquer-trees.
We will cut them to make *qin se*.[68]

Climb up to the old parapets,
And look down over Chu.
Over the Chu hill, the Tang hill,
The Jing hill, the Jing mound.
Go down and see the mulberry fields.
The oracle foretells auspicious,
All truly good.

A blessing rain has come.
Order the head groom
To ready the carriages early by starlight.
We will rest at the mulberry fields.
Our lord is not an ordinary human,[69]
His deliberation far-reaching and deep,
This land of three thousand steeds and mares.

---

[67] This is a poem celebrating the rebuilding of the palace of the court of Wei, after two years of its evacuation from the capital because of the invasion from the north by the Di tribes.

[68] On *qin se*, see note 2.

[69] This line refers to Duke Wen of Wei, during whose rule the court recovers from its years of intrigue and corruption. With the help of Duke Huan of Qi, he is building a new capital on the hill of Chu.

51. 蝃蝀

蝃蝀在東
莫之敢指
女子有行
遠兄弟父母

朝隮于西
崇朝其雨
女子有行
遠兄弟父母

乃如之人也
懷昏姻也
大無信也
不知命也

51. Rainbow

The rainbow in the east,
Nobody dares point at it.
A girl goes away to be married,
Leaving behind her parents and brothers.

The morning rainbow in the west
Brings rain till noon.
A girl goes away to be married,
Leaving behind her parents and brothers.[70]

But a girl like this
Longs for marriage.
She is not to be trusted,
She doesn't know her lot.

---

[70] I read the first two verses of this poem as lines citing two common sayings: the first two lines in each verse concern the rainbow, and the last two in each verse are about the girl's marriage. The third verse is clearly a warning against a girl who is too eager to get married. A word about a common belief about the rainbow in ancient China. The rainbow was then seen as the phenomenon of love-making between Heaven and Earth, to which one was not to pay special attention. The last verse may be read as referring to a girl who shows too much interest in this phenomenon.

52. 相鼠

相鼠有皮
人而無儀
人而無儀
不死何為

相鼠有齒
人而無止
人而無止
不死何俟

相鼠有體
人而無禮
人而無禮
胡不遄死

52. Look at the Rat

Look at the rat, it has a skin.
A man without etiquette,
A man without etiquette,
What is he doing without dying?

Look at the rat, it has teeth.
A man without decency,
A man without decency,
What is he waiting for without dying?

Look at the rat, it has a body.
A man without propriety,
A man without propriety,
Why doesn't he die quickly?

53. 干旄

子子干旄
在浚之郊
素絲紕之
良馬四之
彼姝者子
何以畀之

子子干旟
在浚之都
素絲組之
良馬五之
彼姝者子
何以予之

子子干旌
在浚之城
素絲祝之
良馬六之
彼姝者子
何以告之

53. Pole-banners

High rise the pole-banners[71]
In the field outside Jun.
The reins of white silk braided,
Four fine horses.
That handsome gentleman,
What shall we offer him?

High rise the pole-banners
In the city of Jun.
The reins of white silk plaited,
Five fine horses.
That handsome gentleman,
What shall we give him?

High rise the pole-banners
In the castle of Jun,
The reins of white silk twined,
Six fine horses.
That handsome gentleman,
How shall we speak to him?

---

[71] Note that this song (in the original) mentions three different types of pole-banners: (1) a banner with a line of oxtail tips attached to the pole top, (2) a banner with figures of hawks drawn on it, (3) a banner with a string of bird feathers attached to the pole top. (See Takata, 218).

54. 載馳

載馳載驅
歸唁衛侯

驅馬悠悠
言至于漕
大夫跋涉

我心則憂

既不我嘉
不能旋反
視而不臧
我思不遠

既不我嘉
不能旋濟
視而不臧
我思不閟

陟彼阿丘
言采其虻
女子善懷
亦各有行
許人尤之
眾穉且狂

54. Gallop, Gallop[72]

Gallop, gallop,
I must go home to console the Duke of
    Wei.
Gallop my horses day and night,
To reach Cao.
The Great Officers are after me, crossing the
    fields!
This worries me.

You disagree with me,
I cannot return home.
I see you all displeased,
But my thoughts won't go away.

You disagree with me,
I cannot return home.
I see you all displeased,
But my thoughts won't stop.

I climb that mound
And pick the *meng*.[73]
Women worry too much,
Yet each has her way to go.
The people of Xu find fault with me,
They are childish and mad.

---

[72] Older commentaries universally attribute this poem to the wife of Duke Mu
of Xu, one of the smaller states of the time. According to the *Zuo Chuan*, when
the capital of Wei was invaded by the Di tribes, Lady Mu, being a sister of the
Duke of Wei, wanted to visit her brother in Cao, where he had moved to, but
couldn't return to Wei because of the opposition from the ministers of Xu. One
may read the second verse and the rest as Lady Mu's objection to the ministers.
[73] Waley translates *meng* as "toad-lilies." This plant was believed to help relieve
sadness.

我行其野	I walk in the field,
芃芃其麥	How tall the wheat grows.
控于大邦	Would I appeal to the great state of Qi?[74]
誰因誰極	Whom could I dispatch and to whom?
大夫君子	Oh, Great Officers, gentlemen,
無我有尤	Don't find fault with me.
百爾所思	What you all think
不如我所之	Isn't equal to what I have in mind.

---

[74] Lady Mu was one of the children born between Lady Xuan (the widow of Duke Xuan) and Wan, one of her step sons (see note 63 above). Her mother coming originally from Qi, she must have thought of appealing to the Duke of Qi for help. Note that Duke Huan of Qi did help Duke Wen of Wei rebuild his capital (see note 69).

V. 衛風　Wei Feng[75]

---

[75] For the chapter title see note 35 on the title of Chapter III. Note that the songs in the two preceding chapters are also from the state of Wei. The reader will later also come across the title "Wei Feng" for Chapter IX, which refers to songs from another state Wei. The character for this state is different from the character for *wei* in the present chapter. Though the two characters are today pronounced the same with the same tone, I conjecture that they did sound differently in ancient times.

55. 淇奧

55. The Cove of the Qi

瞻彼淇奧
綠竹猗猗
有匪君子
如切如磋
如琢如磨
瑟兮僩兮
赫兮咺兮
有匪君子
終不可諼兮

Look at that cove of the Qi,
How lush grows the green bamboo!
Elegant is our lord.[76]
As ivory cut and filed,
As jade chiseled and polished.
How gracious, how magnanimous!
How splendorous, how majestic!
Elegant is our lord.
He will never be forgotten.

瞻彼淇奧
綠竹青青
有匪君子
充耳琇瑩
會弁如星
瑟兮僩兮
赫兮咺兮
有匪君子
終不可諼兮

Look at that cove of the Qi,
How luxuriant grows the green bamboo!
Elegant is our lord.
His ear-plugs with gems,
The jades on his cap like stars.
How gracious, how magnanimous!
How splendorous, how majestic!
Elegant is our lord.
He will never be forgotten.

瞻彼淇奧
綠竹如簀
有匪君子
如金如錫
如圭如璧
寬兮綽兮
猗重較兮
善戲謔兮
不為虐兮

Look at that cove of the Qi,
How dense grows the green bamboo!
Elegant is our lord.
Like gold, like silver,
Like *gui*, like *bi*.[77]
How broad-spirited, how easygoing,
He is leaning to the chariot-rail.
He is so playful,
But never cruel.

---

[76] Refers to Duke Wu, one of the early lords of Wei. This poem sings the illustrious virtue of the duke.

[77] Both *gui* and *bi* are pieces of jade used on ritual occasions: *gui* a rectangular tablet and *bi* a round disk.

56. 考槃

考槃在澗
碩人之寬
獨寐寤言
永矢弗諼

考槃在阿
碩人之薖
獨寐寤歌
永矢弗過

考槃在陸
碩人之軸
獨寐寤宿
永矢弗告

56. Joy in the Gully[78]

Joy in the gully,
How broad-spirited is this wise man!
Alone sleeping, awake he says to himself,
He swears never to forget the joy.

Joy on the hillside,
How light-spirited is this wise man!
Alone sleeping, awake he sings,
He swears never to part with the joy.

Joy in the highland.
How carefree is this wise man!
Alone sleeping, awake he remains in bed,
He swears never to tell others the joy.

---

[78] This song is commonly read as a song of a recluse.

57. 碩人

碩人其頎
衣錦褧衣
齊侯之子
衛侯之妻
東宮之妹
邢侯之姨
譚公維私

手如柔荑
膚如凝脂
領如蝤蠐
齒如瓠犀
螓首蛾眉
巧笑倩兮
美目盼兮

碩人敖敖
說于農郊
四牡有驕
朱幩鑣鑣
翟茀以朝

大夫夙退
無使君勞

57. Splendid Woman[79]

This splendid woman, tall,
Wearing brocade under a thin coat,
Daughter of the Lord of Qi,
Wife of the Lord of Wei,[80]
Sister of the Crown Prince of Qi,
Sister-in-law of the Lord of Xing.
The Lord of Tan is her brother-in-law.

Hands white like the reed-ears,
Skin smooth like lard,
Neck long and white like the tree-grub,
Teeth like melon seeds,
Noble forehead, beautiful eyebrows.
Dimples on her smiling face,
Eyes clear and cool.

Festively, this splendid woman
Camps in the field outside the city.
Her four steeds stomp,
Their red bit trappings flutter.
Inside pheasant feather screens[81] she rides to the palace.
Please Great Officers retire early,
Do not tire out our lord.

---

[79] This poem describes the arrival of the bride of Duke Zhang.
[80] I.e., Duke Zhang.
[81] On her carriage.

河水洋洋　　How vast the water of the Huang He,
北流活活　　How forcefully it flows north.
施罛濊濊　　The fish-net swirls,
鱣鮪發發　　Carp and sturgeon leap wild.
葭菼揭揭　　Tall grow reeds and sedges.
庶姜孽孽　　All the Jiang maidens[82] finely coifed,
庶士有朅　　All her knights waiting valiantly!

---

[82] *Jiang* is the clan name of the bride. She is being accompanied on this trip by
girls from her clan.

58. 氓

氓之蚩蚩
抱布貿絲
匪來貿絲
來即我謀
送子涉淇
至于頓丘
匪來愆期
子無良媒
將子無怒
秋以為期
乘彼垝垣
以望復關

不見復關
泣涕漣漣
既見復關
載笑載言
爾卜爾筮
體無咎言
以爾車來
以我賄遷

58. Vendor[83]

A vendor came smiling meekly,
He carried cloth to trade for thread.
Not to trade for thread,
But to talk me into marrying him.
Escorting you, I crossed the Qi,
As far as Dunqiu.
"It's not that I want to put it off,
You don't have a proper match-maker.
Please don't be angry,
I propose autumn as our time."
I climbed that ruined wall
To see you come through the gate.

When I didn't see you there,
My tears streamed down.
When I saw you there,
We happily chatted and laughed.
"You consult your yarrow-stalks,
And if the sign shows nothing ill-boding,
You will come with your cart,
And I will take my things and go with you."

---

[83] Shrakawa's reading of the title (*wang*) is as "vendor" (214). The basic meaning of the character *wang* is "folk," with the connotation of "wandering" people.

桑之未落	The mulberry leaves, while on the trees,
其葉沃若	How tender and lustrous they are!
于嗟鳩兮	Oh doves,
無食桑葚	Don't eat mulberries.[84]
于嗟女兮	Ah, girls,
無與士耽	Don't indulge in pleasure with young men.
士之耽兮	Men's indulgence
猶可說也	May still be excused,
女之耽兮	Girls' indulgence
不可說也	Never to be excused.
桑之落矣	The mulberry leaves falling,
其黃而隕	Ah, yellow and withered.
自我徂爾	Since I came to you,
三歲食貧	For three years, I have lived in poverty.
淇水湯湯	The waters of the Qi, rising high,
漸車帷裳	Wetted the curtains of my carriage.[85]
女也不爽	The woman has never failed in her duties,
士貳其行	But the man has neglected his.
士也罔極	He has been licentious,
二三其德	His behavior capricious.

---

[84] It was believed that the berries would intoxicate the birds and make them ill.

[85] The wetting of the curtains in crossing waters to be married was considered an ill omen.

三歲為婦
靡室勞矣
夙興夜寐
靡有朝矣
言既遂矣
至于暴矣
兄弟不知
咥其笑矣
靜言思之
躬自悼矣

及爾偕老
老使我怨
淇則有岸
隰則有泮
總角之宴
言笑晏晏
信誓旦旦
不思其反
反是不思
亦已焉哉

For three years, as your wife,
I have never spared my labor.
Rising early, going to bed late at night,
No moment of rest.
Once our life got easier,
You began to be violent to me.
My brothers don't recognize my troubles,
They laugh and laugh.
Calmly thinking of all this,
I only feel sorry for myself.

To be your companion till death,
Growing old makes me feel resentful.
The Qi has its banks,
The swamp has its shores.
How joyous we were before our marriage,
You talked and laughed so gaily.
You swore to be true,
I didn't think you would change.
I never thought of this betrayal,
Ah, it's all over for me!

59. 竹竿

蘀蘀竹竿
以釣于淇
豈不爾思
遠莫致之

泉源在左
淇水在右
女子有行
遠兄弟父母

淇水在右
泉源在左
巧笑之瑳
佩玉之儺

淇水滺滺
檜楫松舟
駕言出遊
以寫我憂

59. Bamboo Rod

How pliant that bamboo rod!
You were fishing at the Qi.
How can I help thinking of you?
You are so far away, I cannot reach you.

The Quan on the left,
The Qi on the right.
A girl goes away to get married,
Leaving behind her parents and brothers.

The Qi on the right,
The Quan on the left.
Your sweet smile, those white teeth,
Your girdle-gems, that soft sound!

Slowly flow the waters of the Qi,
Oars of juniper, boat of pine.
Get the carriage ready for a ride,
That I may be rid of my sadness.

60. 芄蘭

芄蘭之支	A vine-bean branch,
童子佩觿	The boy carries a knot-awl at his belt.
雖則佩觿	Though he carries a knot-awl at his belt,
能不我知	He fails to recognize me.[86]
容兮遂兮	Affected, arrogant,
垂帶悸兮	His belt ends are dangling.
芄蘭之葉	A vine-bean leave,
童子佩韘	The boy carries an archer's glove at his belt.
雖則佩韘	Though he carries an archer's glove at his belt,
能不我甲	He fails to befriend me.
容兮遂兮	Affected, arrogant,
垂帶悸兮	His belt ends are dangling.

60. Vine-bean

---

[86] Shirakawa reads *wo* (the first-person pronoun) in this line as a woman who laughs at a boy who pretends to be a man but fails to show any interest in women (218).

84

61. 河廣

61. The Broad Huang He[87]

誰謂河廣
一葦杭之
誰謂宋遠
跂予望之

Who says the Huang He is broad?
On a single reed you can cross it.
Who says Song[88] is far away?
Standing on tip-toe, I can see it.

誰謂河廣
曾不容刀
誰謂宋遠
曾不崇朝

Who says the Huang He is broad?
It won't hold a cutter.
Who says Song is far away?
You may get there before breakfast.

---

[87] Traditionally this poem has been read as one sung by a sister of Duke Wen of Wei, who was longing to see her son, who had become the Duke of Song, succeeding his father, Duke Huan. But one may easily read it as a song by a woman of Wei longing to see her lover in Song.
[88] The state of Song far to the south from Wei.

62. 伯兮

伯兮朅兮
邦之桀兮
伯也執殳
為王前驅

自伯之東
首如飛蓬
豈無膏沐
誰適為容

其雨其雨
杲杲出日
願言思伯
甘心首疾

焉得諼草
言樹之背
願言思伯
使我心痗

62. You Are a Brave One

Oh, my dear, you are a brave one.
Bravest warrior in this land.
A lance in your hand,
Outrider for the king.

Since you went to the east,
My hair has turned wild like tumbleweed,
Not that I lack hair oil,
For whom would I make up?

Will it rain, will it?
The dazzling sun instead.
Longing, I think of you,
My mind weary, my head in pain.

Where could I get the forget-all grass?
I would plant it behind the house.
Longing, I think of you,
This hurts my heart.

63. 有狐

有狐綏綏
在彼淇梁
心之憂矣
之子無裳

有狐綏綏
在彼淇厲
心之憂矣
之子無帶

有狐綏綏
在彼淇側
心之憂矣
之子無服。

63. Fox Dragging About

A fox is dragging about
By the fish-weir on the Qi.
I am worried,
This girl has no skirt on.[89]

A fox is dragging about
By the ford on the Qi.
I am worried,
This girl has no belt on.

A fox is dragging about
On the shore of the Qi.
I am worried,
This girl has no clothes on.

---

[89] I translate *zhi zi* as "this girl," following Shirakawa's reading (223). Usually the two characters are read as "this man." Obviously, the circumstance of the poem is unclear. Why has this person no skirt, no belt, and indeed no clothes on? In spite of the widely varying interpretations of this line, all agree on the implication of a male fox roving around to find his mate.

64. 木瓜

投我以木瓜
報之以瓊琚
匪報也
永以為好也

投我以木桃
報之以瓊瑤
匪報也
永以為好也

投我以木李
報之以瓊玖
匪報也
永以為好也

64. Quince

She threw me a quince,[90]
In return I gave her a red *ju* jade.[91]
Not in return,
But to show my love to her forever.

She threw me a peach,
In return I gave her a fine *yao* jade.
Not in return,
But to show my love to her forever.

She threw me a plum,
In return I gave her a dark *jiu* jade.
Not in return,
But to show my love to her forever.

---

[90] See note 22.

[91] This song mentions three different kinds of jade (*ju*, *yao*, and *jiu*), all precious stones for girdle.

VI. 王風　Wang Feng[92]

---

[92] This chapter contains songs from Loyang and its surrounding areas. The original capital of the Zhou dynasty, Hao, had been invaded by the northern tribes, bringing the Western Zhou to an end, and the Eastern Zhou, with the enthronement of King Ping, began in the new capital, Loyang, in 770 BCE. Wang in the chapter title refers to this royal domain.

65. 黍離

65. The Millet Bending

彼黍離離
彼稷之苗
行邁靡靡
中心搖搖
知我者
謂我心憂
不知我者
謂我何求
悠悠蒼天
此何人哉

That millet is bending,
That sorghum is sprouting
I walk on and on, my steps heavy,
My mind is adrift.
Those who know me
Say I am worried.
Those who don't know me
Ask what is he seeking?
Oh, that limitless blue sky,
Who is this man?

彼黍離離
彼稷之穗
行邁靡靡
中心如醉
知我者
謂我心憂
不知我者
謂我何求
悠悠蒼天
此何人哉

That millet is bending,
That sorghum is coming into ear.
I walk on and on, my steps heavy,
My mind is swaying as if drunk.
Those who know me
Say I am worried.
Those who don't know me
Ask what is he seeking?
Oh, that limitless blue sky,
Who is this man?

彼黍離離
彼稷之實
行邁靡靡
中心如噎
知我者
謂我心憂
不知我者
謂我何求
悠悠蒼天
此何人哉

That millet is bending,
That sorghum is bearing grain.
I walk on and on, my steps heavy,
My heart is choking.
Those who know me
Say I am worried.
Those who don't know me
Ask what is he seeking?
Oh, that limitless blue sky,
Who is this man?

66. 君子于役

君子于役
不知其期
曷至哉
雞棲于塒
日之夕矣
羊牛下來
君子于役
如之何勿思

君子于役
不日不月
曷其有佸
雞棲于桀
日之夕矣
羊牛下括
君子于役
苟無飢渴

66. He Is Gone to Service[93]

He is gone to service.
I don't know how long,
Oh, when will he come?
The chickens are gone to roost,
Another evening,
The sheep and cows are coming down.
He is gone to service,
How can I help thinking of him?

He is gone to service,
What day, which month,
When will I see him?
The chickens are on their perches.
Another evening,
The sheep and cows are down.
He is gone to service,
I hope he doesn't go hungry and thirsty.

---

[93] By *jun zi* in this song and the next, the speaker is referring to her husband.
(See Shirakawa, 233; Takata, 272).

67. 君子陽陽

君子陽陽
左執簧
右招我由房
其樂只且

君子陶陶
左執翿
右招我由敖

其樂只且

67. How Merry He Was[94]

How merry he was!
The *huang* organ[95] in his left hand,
With his right hand he invited me to join.
How joyful we were!

So carefree he was!
The dancing plume in his left hand,
With his right hand he invited me to
    dance.
How joyful we were!

---

[94] See note 93.
[95] The *huang* is a woodwind instrument (consisting of a series of small bamboo pipes), usually translated as "mouth organ" or "small pipe organ."

68. 揚之水

68. Spraying Stream

揚之水	The spraying stream[96]
不流束薪	Fails to carry off the bundle of firewood.
彼其之子	Ah, that girl,
不與我戍申	Away from her, I am defending Shen.
懷哉	How I miss her!
懷哉	How I miss her!
曷月予還歸哉	In what month shall I return?
揚之水	The spraying stream
不流束楚	Fails to carry off the bundle of brushwood.
彼其之子	Ah, that girl,
不與我戍甫	Away from her, I am defending Fu.
懷哉	How I miss her!
懷哉	How I miss her!
曷月予還歸哉	In what month shall I return?
揚之水	The spraying stream
不流束蒲	Fails to carry off the bundle of rushes.
彼其之子	Ah, that girl,
不與我戍許	Away from her, I am defending Xu.
懷哉	How I miss her!
懷哉	How I miss her!
曷月予還歸哉	In what month shall I return?

---

[96] In the *Shi Jing* there are three songs that begin with this phrase "the spraying stream" (*yang zhi shui*). In two of them (Nos. 68 and 92), this first line is followed also by the identical second line except for a single variant ("Fails to carry off the bundle of firewood [briers]"). These two lines (and their minor variations) are variously read, which often result in different translations. I follow here Shirakawa, who interprets them as a reading of divination by a "spraying stream," a sort of hydromancy, in which one tells whether or not one's wish or hope will be fulfilled by watching how the flow of the stream carries a small bundle of branches or rushes. If the bundle is carried off, the omen is good, if not, the omen is bad. (See 237, and also Shirakawa, *Shi Kyō*, 22–24).

69. 中谷有蓷　　69. Motherwort in the Valley

中谷有蓷　　　　The motherwort in the valley,
暵其乾矣　　　　Withered and dry.
有女仳離　　　　A woman, by herself,
慨其歎矣　　　　Bitterly grieves,
慨其歎矣　　　　Bitterly grieves.
遇人之艱難矣　　She has met her husband's ill fortune.

中谷有蓷　　　　The motherwort in the valley,
暵其脩矣　　　　Withered and hanging.
有女仳離　　　　A woman, by herself,
條其嘯矣　　　　Long sighs,
慨其嘯矣　　　　Long sighs.
遇人之不淑矣　　She has met the death of her husband.[97]

中谷有蓷　　　　The motherwort in the valley,
暵其濕矣　　　　Withered and wilted.
有女仳離　　　　A woman, by herself,
啜其泣矣　　　　Sobbing,
啜其泣矣　　　　Sobbing,
何嗟及矣　　　　What good would the lament bring her?

---

[97] Shirakawa's reading (239).

70. 兔爰

有兔爰爰
雉離于羅
我生之初
尚無為
我生之後
逢此百罹
尚寐無吪

有兔爰爰
雉離于罦
我生之初
尚無造
我生之後
逢此百憂
尚寐無覺

有兔爰爰
雉離于罿
我生之初
尚無庸
我生之後
逢此百凶
尚寐無聰

70. The Carefree Hare

Carefree the hare goes around,
Caught in the net is a pheasant.
At my birth
The world was still quiet.
Since my birth
We have met these hundred plagues.
Would that I might sleep and wake no more.

Carefree the hare goes around,
Caught in the trap is a pheasant.
At my birth
The world was still at peace.
Since my birth
We have met these hundred disasters.
Would that I might sleep and feel no more.

Carefree the hare goes around,
Caught in the trap is a pheasant.
At my birth
The world was still calm.
Since my birth
We have met these hundred woes.
Would that I might sleep and hear no more.

71. 葛藟

緜緜葛藟
在河之滸
終遠兄弟
謂他人父
謂他人父
亦莫我顧

緜緜葛藟
在河之涘
終遠兄弟
謂他人母
謂他人母
亦莫我有

緜緜葛藟
在河之漘
終遠兄弟
謂他人昆
謂他人昆
亦莫我聞

71. Creepers

Long, long spread the creepers
Along the shores of the river.
I have come far away from my brothers.
I call a stranger Father,
I call a stranger Father.
Yet he isn't gentle to me.

Long, long spread the creepers
Along the sides of the river.
I have come far away from my brothers.
I call a stranger Mother,
I call a stranger Mother.
Yet she isn't kind to me.

Long, long spread the creepers
Along the banks of the river.
I have come far away from my brothers.
I call strangers sisters,
I call strangers sisters.
Yet they don't listen to me.

72. 采葛

彼采葛兮
一日不見
如三月兮

彼采蕭兮
一日不見
如三秋兮

彼采艾兮
一日不見
如三歲兮

72. Pluck the Cloth-creepers

Pluck, pluck the cloth-creepers.
Not seeing him a single day,
It's like three months.

Pluck, pluck the wormwood.
Not seeing him a single day,
It's like three autumns.

Pluck, pluck the mugwort.
Not seeing him a single day,
It's like three years.

73. 大車

大車檻檻
毳衣如菼
豈不爾思
畏子不敢

大車哼哼
毳衣如璊
豈不爾思
畏子不奔

穀則異室
死則同穴
謂予不信
有如皦日。

73. Great Carriage

Your great carriage rolling,
Your woolen coat green as reed.
How can I help thinking of you?
I fear approaching you.[98]

Your great carriage rumbling,
Your woolen coat red as *wan* jade.
How can I help thinking of you?
I fear going with you.

Alive, we are separate,
Dead, we will share the same grave.
You don't trust my words?
I swear before the bright sun.

---

[98] Shirakawa suggests that this is probably a song by a lowly woman who secretly loves a man of higher standing (246).

74. 丘中有麻

74. On the Hill Grows the Hemp

丘中有麻
彼留子嗟
彼留子嗟
將其來施

On the hill grows the hemp.
Ah, that Zijue of Liu,
Ah, that Zijue of Liu,
If only he would visit me.

丘中有麥
彼留子國
彼留子國
將其來食

On the hill grows the wheat.
Ah, that Ziguo of Liu,
Ah, that Ziguo of Liu,
If only he would come for a meal.

丘中有李
彼留之子
彼留之子
貽我佩玖

On the hill grow plum-trees.
Ah, that young man of Liu,
Ah, that young man of Liu,
If only he would send me a girdle jade!

22

VII. 鄭風 Zheng Feng[99]

[99] This chapter contains songs from the state of Zheng, further to the east of Loyang. Historically, the "songs of Zheng" have been regarded as "immoral" or "licentious," especially because of Confucius's unfavorable remark ("The voice of Zheng lecherous").

75. 緇衣

緇衣之宜兮
敝予又改為兮
適子之館兮
還予授子之粲兮

緇衣之好兮
敝予又改造兮
適子之館兮
還予授子之粲兮

緇衣之蓆兮
敝予又改作兮
適子之館兮
還予授子之粲兮

75. Black Coat[100]

How well your black coat fits!
When it frays, I will make a new one.
Now you go to your office,
When you return, I will serve you fine
food.

How nice your black coat looks!
When it frays, I will make a new one.
Now you go to your office,
When you return, I will serve you fine
food.

How elegant your black coat is!
When it frays, I will make a new one.
Now you go to your office,
When you return, I will serve you fine
food.

---

[100] In the original, one finds hardly any change in the three verses of this song in meaning or imagery. In their first two lines, a single character is changed, but without shifting in meaning. I follow Takata's reading (301–2). Shirakawa suggests that "fine food" in the last line of each verse means rather an unsubtle way in which the singing woman is seducing the man in the black coat (253).

76. 將仲子

將仲子兮
無踰我里
無折我樹杞

豈敢愛之
畏我父母
仲可懷也
父母之言
亦可畏也

將仲子兮
無踰我牆
無折我樹桑

豈敢愛之
畏我諸兄
仲可懷也
諸兄之言
亦可畏也

將仲子兮
無踰我園
無折我樹檀

豈敢愛之
畏人之多言
仲可懷也
人之多言
亦可畏也

76. Please, Zhongzi

Please, Zhongzi,
Don't climb over the village wall,
Don't break the willow-trees we have
      planted.
Not that I am concerned with them,
I am afraid of my parents.
I love you, Zhongzi,
But I am afraid
Of what my parents will say.

Please, Zhongzi,
Don't climb over our fence,
Don't break the mulberry-trees we have
      planted.
Not that I am concerned with them,
I am afraid of my brothers.
I love you, Zhonzi,
But I am afraid
Of what my brothers will say.

Please, Zhongzi,
Don't climb into our garden,
Don't break the spindle trees we have
      planted.
Not that I am concerned with them,
I am afraid of what people say.
I love you, Zhongzi,
But I am afraid
Of what people will say.

77. 叔于田

叔于田
巷無居人
豈無居人
不如叔也
洵美且仁

叔于狩
巷無飲酒
豈無飲酒
不如叔也
洵美且好

叔適野
巷無服馬
豈無服馬
不如叔也
洵美且武

77. Shu Goes to the Hunting-fields (1)

Shu is gone to the hunting-fields.
In our village nobody is around.
Not that nobody is around,
None is like Shu,
So handsome, so kind.

Shu is gone hunting.
In our village nobody drinks wine.
Not that nobody drinks wine,
None is like Shu,
So handsome, so friendly.

Shu is gone to the fields.
In our village nobody drives horses.
Not that nobody drives horses,
None is like Shu,
So handsome, so brave.

78. 大叔于田

78. Shu Goes to the Hunting-fields (2)[101]

叔于田	Shu goes to the hunting-fields,
乘乘馬	Driving his team of four horses.
執轡如組	He holds the reins as if ribbons,
兩驂如舞	The two side-horses running as if dancing.
叔在藪	Shu arriving in the prairie,
火烈具舉	The flames rise high all around.
襢裼暴虎	Bare-armed, he attacks a tiger,
獻于公所	He brings it to the Duke's place.
將叔無狃	Please, Shu, don't be rash,
戒其傷女	Be careful, you may be hurt.
叔于田	Shu goes to the hunting-fields,
乘乘黃	Driving his team of bays.
兩服上襄	The two yoke-horses ahead,
兩驂雁行	The two side-horses keep abreast.
叔在藪	Shu arriving in the prairie,
火烈具揚	The flames leap high all around.
叔善射忌	How well Shu shoots!
又良御忌	How well he drives!
抑磬控忌	Now giving rein, now pulling rein,
抑縱送忌	Now letting arrows fly, now pursuing game.
叔于田	Shu goes to the hunting-fields,
乘乘鴇	Driving his team of grays.
兩服齊首	The two yoke-horses with heads in line,
兩驂如手	The two side-horses running as if hands moving.
叔在藪	Shu arriving in the prairie,
火烈具阜	The flames flare up all around.
叔馬慢忌	His horses slowing down,
叔發罕忌	Shu shoots less and less.
抑釋掤忌	Now, he closes his quiver,
抑鬯弓忌	Now, he puts his bow in its case.

---

[101] The Chinese title of this song has the character *da* (meaning "large") added to that of the preceding poem, to be distinguished from it.

79. 清人　79. Men of Qing

清人在彭	The men of Qing are in Peng,
駟介旁旁	The teams of four armored horses, milling around.
二矛重英	Two spears flying red plumes, one over the other,
河上乎翱翔	On the shores of the Huang He they roam.
清人在消	The men of Qing are in Xiao,
駟介麃麃	The teams of four armored horses look fearsome.
二矛重喬	Two spears flying pheasant feathers, one over the other,
河上乎逍遙	On the shores of the Huang He they ramble.
清人在軸	The men of Qing are in Zhou,
駟介陶陶	The teams of four armored horses, resting at ease.
左旋右抽	The Left troops circling around, the Right troops pulling their arrows,
中軍作好	The Center enjoying themselves.

80. 羔裘

羔裘如濡
洵直且侯
彼其之子
舍命不渝

羔裘豹飾
孔武有力
彼其之子
邦之司直

羔裘晏兮
三英粲兮
彼其之子
邦之彦兮

80. Lamb Coat

His lamb coat lustrous,
Truly he is upright and lordly.
That gentleman
Abides by his duty, never wavering.

His lamb coat, sleeved with leopard's fur,
He is brave and strong.
That gentleman
Is the upholder of justice in our land.

His lamb coat so splendid,
His three flowery tufts so brilliant.
That gentleman
Is a pillar of our land.

81. 遵大路

遵大路兮
摻執子之袪兮
無我惡兮
不寁故也

遵大路兮
摻執子之手兮
無我醜兮
不寁好也

81. On the Main Road

On the main road,
If I come along to hold of your sleeve,
Do not hate me.
Please do not ignore your bygone friend.

On the main road,
If I come along to grasp your hand,
Do not detest me.
Please do not ignore your bygone love.

82. 女曰雞鳴

82. The Woman Says "The Cock Has Crowed"

女曰雞鳴
士曰昧旦
子興視夜
明星有爛
將翱將翔
弋鳧與雁

The woman says, "The cock has crowed."
The man says, "It isn't bright yet."
"Get up and look at the sky."
"The morning star is shining."
"Please up and get busy out in the field,
Shoot the duck and geese."

弋言加之
與子宜之
宜言飲酒
與子偕老
琴瑟在御
莫不靜好

Catch them,
I will prepare a fine dish for you.
We will drink wine with it.
Till death we shall share our life,
Qin se[102] by our sides.
We will live happily in peace.

知子之來之
雜佩以贈之
知子之順之
雜佩以問之
知子之好之
雜佩以報之

Knowing you will come to me,[103]
I will send you girdles of assorted stones.
Knowing you will be tender to me,
I will give you girdles of assorted stones.
Knowing you will love me,
In return, I will send you girdles of
assorted stones.

---

[102] *Qin* and *se*, two common musical instruments. See note 2.

[103] In this stanza, the woman repeatedly tells the man that she would send him "girdles of assorted stones." She is promising him her marriage to him. See Shirakawa, 268.

83. 有女同車

有女同車
顏如舜華
將翱將翔
佩玉瓊琚
彼美孟姜
洵美且都

有女同行
顏如舜英
將翱將翔
佩玉將將
彼美孟姜
德音不忘

83. Girl Riding with Me

A girl rides a carriage with me,
Her face like a hibiscus flower.
We ride and ride everywhere,
Her girdle-gems, red and black.
That beautiful Jiang sister,
Truly fair and elegant.

A girl rides a carriage with me,
Her face like a rose of Sharon.
We ride and ride everywhere,
Her girdle-gems jingling.
That beautiful Jiang sister,
Her lovely voice unforgettable.

84. 山有扶蘇　　84. On the Hill Grows the *Fusu*

山有扶蘇　　　　On the hill grows the *fusu*,[104]
隰有荷華　　　　In the wetland grows the lotus flower.
不見子都　　　　I don't see a Zidou,[105]
乃見狂且　　　　Instead, I see this madman.

山有喬松　　　　On the hill grows the tall pine,
隰有游龍　　　　In the wetland grows the smartweed.
不見子充　　　　I don't see a Zichong,[106]
乃見狡童　　　　Instead, I see this sly boy.

---

[104] A tree unidentifiable. Waley translates it as "nutgrass".
[105] The name Zidou refers to a handsome man.
[106] Zichong refers to a decent man.

85. 蘀兮

蘀兮
蘀兮
風其吹女
叔兮伯兮
倡予和女

蘀兮
蘀兮
風其漂女
叔兮伯兮
倡予要女

85. Oh, Falling Leaves

Oh, falling leaves,
Falling leaves,
The wind blows you away.
Oh, men, young and old,
Set the tune, I will follow you.

Oh, falling leaves,
Falling leaves,
The wind carries you away.
Oh, men, young and old,
Set the tune, I will answer you.

86. 狡童

彼狡童兮
不與我言兮
維子之故
使我不能餐兮

彼狡童兮
不與我食兮
維子之故
使我不能息兮

86. Mean Fellow

Oh, that mean fellow,
He wouldn't speak to me.
Only because of you,
I can hardly swallow food.

Oh, that mean fellow,
He wouldn't eat with me.
Only because of you,
I can hardly breathe.

87. 褰裳

87. Tucking up the Dress

子惠思我
褰裳涉溱

If you love me,
I shall tuck up the dress and wade across the
    Qin.

子不我思
豈無他人
狂童之狂也且

If you don't think of me,
Aren't there other men?
Oh, you are deluded!

子惠思我
褰裳涉洧

If you love me,
I shall tuck up the dress and wade across the
    Wei.

子不我思
豈無他士
狂童之狂也且

If you don't think of me,
Aren't there other young men?
Oh, you are deluded!

88. 丰

子之丰兮
俟我乎巷兮
悔予不送兮

子之昌兮
俟我乎堂兮
悔予不將兮

衣錦褧衣
裳錦褧裳
叔兮伯兮
駕予與行

裳錦褧裳
衣錦褧衣
叔兮伯兮
駕予與歸

88. How Gorgeous

How gorgeous that man!
He waited for me in the lane,
I regret I didn't send him off.

How splendid that man!
He waited for me in the hall.
I regret I didn't go with him.

In my brocaded dress
Under a thin frock,
Oh, uncles,
Get the carriage ready, I will go with him.

Under a thin frock,
In my brocaded dress
Oh, uncles,
Get the carriage ready, I will go to marry
    him.

89. 東門之墠

東門之墠
茹藘在阪
其室則邇
其人甚遠

東門之栗
有踐家室
豈不爾思
子不我即

89. By the Clearing at the East Gate

By the clearing at the East Gate
The madder grows on the slope.
His house is so near,
He is so distant.

By the chestnut trees at the East Gate
There stand houses in a row.
How can I help thinking of you?
You don't approach me.

90. 風雨

風雨淒淒
雞鳴喈喈
既見君子
云胡不夷

風雨瀟瀟
雞鳴膠膠
既見君子
云胡不瘳

風雨如晦
雞鳴不已
既見君子
云胡不喜

90. Windy Rain

Windy rain, fierce,
The chickens are shrieking.
If I saw you,
Wouldn't I be at peace?

Windy rain, furious,
The chickens are screaming.
If I saw you,
Wouldn't I calm down?

Windy rain, darkening,
The chickens won't quit screaming.
If I saw you,
Wouldn't I rejoice?

91. 子衿

青青子衿
悠悠我心
縱我不往
子寧不嗣音

青青子佩
悠悠我思
縱我不往
子寧不來

挑兮達兮
在城闕兮
一日不見
如三月兮

91. Blue Collar

Oh, your collar so blue,
My longing never ceases.
Even though I don't go to you,
How come you don't send me your news?

Oh, your girdle so blue,
My thoughts never end.
Even though I don't go to you,
How come you don't come to me?

Merrily, they are frolicking
At the wall-gate.
Not seeing you a single day,
It's like three months.

92. 揚之水

揚之水
不流束楚
終鮮兄弟
維予與女
無信人之言
人實迋女

揚之水
不流束薪
終鮮兄弟
維予二人
無信人之言
人實不信

92. Spraying Stream

The spraying stream
Doesn't carry off the bundle of briers.[107]
All gone are our brothers,
Only you and I left.
Don't believe what people say,
They are really deceiving you.

The spraying stream
Doesn't carry off the bundle of firewood.
All gone are our brothers,
Only two of us left.
Don't believe what people say.
They are really not to be believed.

---

[107] See note 96.

93. 出其東門

93. Outside the East Gate

出其東門
有女如雲
雖則如雲
匪我思存
縞衣綦巾
聊樂我員

Outside the East Gate
Girls as many as clouds.
Though as many as clouds,
None the one in my thoughts.
Someone in white clothes, blue kerchief
Alone my glad companion.

出其闍闍
有女如荼
雖則如荼
匪我思且
縞衣茹藘
聊可與娛

Outside the East Terrace
Girls as lovely as reed flowers.
Though as lovely as reed flowers,
None the one in my thoughts.
Someone in white clothes, madder color
Alone brings me joy.

94. 野有蔓草

野有蔓草
零露溥兮
有美一人
清揚婉兮
邂逅相遇
適我願兮

野有蔓草
零露瀼瀼
有美一人
婉如清揚
邂逅相遇
與子偕臧

94. In the Field Grow Creepers

In the field grow creepers,
How thick the dew on them.
There is a man beautiful,
His cool look, how lovely!
If we meet by chance,
How glad I will be!

In the field grow creepers,
How heavy the dew on them!
There is a man beautiful,
How lovely his cool look!
If we meet by chance,
We will be happy together!

95. 溱洧

95. The Qin and Wei

溱與洧
方渙渙兮
士與女
方秉蘭兮
女曰觀乎
士曰既且
且往觀乎
洧之外
洵訏且樂
維士與女
伊其相謔
贈之以勺藥

The Qin and Wei
Are flowing in full flood.
Now the young men and women
Are picking the *jian* plant.[108]
The woman says, "Let's go and see,"[109]
The man says, "I already saw it."
"But let's go and see.
The field outside the Wei
Is so open and lovely.
There the young men and women
Are having fun,
Giving each other peonies."

溱與洧
瀏其清矣
士與女
殷其盈兮
女曰觀乎
士曰既且
且往觀乎
洧之外
洵訏且樂
維士與女
伊其將謔
贈之以勺藥

The Qin and Wei,
Are running deep and clear.
Now the young men and women
Are gathering there, all packed.
The woman says, "Let's go and see,"
The man says, "I already saw it."
"But let's go and see.
The field outside the Wei
Is so open and lovely.
There the young men and women
Are having fun,
Giving each other peonies."

---

[108] An aromatic plant.

[109] The woman is asking the man to go to the spring festival in which young men and women gather for merrymaking—dancing, courting, and mating.

VIII. 齊風　Qi Feng[110]

---

[110] This chapter includes songs from Qi, one of the large states of the Zhou dynasty, occupying the eastern part of the kingdom, which includes the present Shandong Province.

123

96. 雞鳴

雞既鳴矣
朝既盈矣
匪雞則鳴
蒼蠅之聲

東方明矣
朝既昌矣
匪東方則明
月出之光

蟲飛薨薨
甘與子同夢
會且歸矣
無庶予子憎

96. The Cock Has Crowed

"The cock has crowed,
The morning light fills the sky."
"It wasn't the cock crowing,
It was the green flies buzzing."

"The eastern sky is bright,
It's broad daylight."
"It isn't the glow of dawn,
It's moonlight."

"The gnats are buzzing around,
How sweet was the dream we shared.
When you meet, you also part.
Hope you will not hate me."

97. 還

子之還兮
遭我乎猺之間兮
並驅從兩肩兮

揖我謂我儇兮

子之茂兮
遭我乎猺之道兮
並驅從兩牡兮
揖我謂我好兮

子之昌兮
遭我乎猺之陽兮
並驅從兩狼兮
揖我謂我臧兮

97. How Quick

How swift you were!
You met me in the hills of Mount Niu.
Side by side we drove, chasing two giant
    boars.
Bowing to me, you said "how nimble."

How strong you were!
You met me on the mountain road of Niu.
Side by side we drove, chasing two stags.
Bowing to me, you said "a good job."

How splendid you were!
You met me on the south slope of Niu.
Side by side we drove, chasing two wolves.
Bowing to me, you said "superb."

98. 著

俟我於著乎而
充耳以素乎而
尚之以瓊華乎而

俟我於庭乎而
充耳以青乎而
尚之以瓊瑩乎而

俟我於堂乎而
充耳以黃乎而
尚之以瓊英乎而

98. Inside the Gate

He was waiting for me inside the gate.
White were his ear-plugs,
Pretty jades shining on them.

He was waiting for me in the courtyard.
Blue were his ear-plugs,
Brilliant jades shining on them.

He was waiting for me in the hall.
Yellow were his ear-plugs,
Beautiful jades shining on them.

99. 東方之日　　99. Sun in the East

東方之日兮　　Sun in the east!
彼姝者子　　This lovely woman
在我室兮　　Is in my house,
在我室兮　　Is in my house.
履我即兮　　Following me, she is with me.[111]

東方之月兮　　Moon in the east!
彼姝者子　　This lovely woman
在我闥兮　　Is in my courtyard,
在我闥兮　　Is in my courtyard.
履我發兮　　Following me, she goes with me.

---

[111] This song is commonly read as an immoral or licentious one. Why not read it as a simple love song?

100. 東方未明　　100. The Eastern Sky Is Still Dark

東方未明　　　　The eastern sky is still dark.
顛倒衣裳　　　　Upside down, he puts on jacket and skirt,
顛之倒之　　　　Upside down, inside out.
自公召之　　　　It's a summons from the lord.

東方未晞　　　　The eastern sky is not yet bright.
顛倒裳衣　　　　Inside out, he puts on skirt and jacket,
倒之顛之　　　　Outside in, downside up.
自公令之　　　　It's a summons from the lord.

折柳樊圃　　　　This mad fellow, helter-skelter,
狂夫瞿瞿　　　　Breaks the willow fences.
不能辰夜　　　　The lord knows nothing of day or night,
不夙則莫　　　　Either too early or too late.

101. 南山

101. South Mountain[112]

南山崔崔	High and steep is the south mountain,
雄狐綏綏	There roams the male fox leisurely.
魯道有蕩	The road to Lu level and broad,
齊子由歸	This way the woman of Qi[113] went to be married.
既曰歸止	Once she went this way,
曷又懷止	Why would anyone again think of her?
葛屨五兩	Cloth-shoes five pairs,
冠緌雙止	Cap-ribbons two pairs.[114]
魯道有蕩	The road to Lu level and broad,
齊子庸止	This way the woman of Qi went to be married.
既曰庸止	Once she took this way,
曷又從止	Why would anyone again follow after her?
蓺麻如之何	How do you plant hemp?
衡從其畝	Across and along you follow the rows.
取妻如之何	How do you take your wife?
必告父母	You must first tell your parents.
既曰告止	Once you have told them,
曷又鞠止	Why would you again pursue any woman?
析薪如之何	How do you cut firewood?
匪斧不克	Without an ax you cannot.
取妻如之何	How do you take your wife?
匪媒不得	Without a match-maker you cannot.
既曰得止	Once you have got your wife,
曷又極止	Why would you again go after another woman?

---

[112] This poem is traditionally read in view of the incestuous relation between the Duke Rang and his sister, Wen Jiang. Wen Jiang was married to Duke Huan of Lu. Duke Rang continued his illicit relation with Wen Jiang even after her marriage.

[113] Wen Jiang.

[114] Marriage gifts?

102. 甫田

無田甫田
維莠驕驕
無思遠人
勞心忉忉

無田甫田
維莠桀桀
無思遠人
勞心怛怛

婉兮孌兮
總角丱兮
未幾見兮
突而弁兮

102. Open Field

Don't till an open field,
Only weeds will grow rampant.
Don't love a man far away,
Your worry will hurt you.

Don't till a large field,
Only weeds will thrive tall.
Don't love a man far away,
Your worry will torment you.

How cute, how adorable was he!
His side-locks bound up.
I haven't seen him in a little while,
Suddenly there he stands in a man's cap.

103. 盧令

盧令令
其人美且仁

盧重環
其人美且鬈

盧重鋂
其人美且偲

103. Black Hound

Here comes a black hound *ling ling*,
His master so handsome, and so kind-
hearted.

The black hound, with double ring,
His master so handsome, and his hair so
beautiful.

The black hound, with triple ring,
His master so handsome, and his beard so
magnificent.

104. 敝笱

敝笱在梁　　　　A broken fish-trap by the weir,
其魚魴鰥　　　　In it swims a large fish.
齊子歸止　　　　The lady from Qi goes home,[116]
其從如雲　　　　Her escort follows like clouds.

敝笱在梁　　　　A broken fish-trap by the weir,
其魚魴鱮　　　　In it swims a large fish.
齊子歸止　　　　The lady from Qi goes home,
其從如雨　　　　Her escort follows like rain.

敝笱在梁　　　　A broken fish-trap by the weir,
其魚唯唯　　　　How free the fish swims in and out.
齊子歸止　　　　The lady from Qi goes home,
其從如水　　　　Her escort follows like a river.

---

[115] This poem is read in the light of Wen Jiang's marriage to Duke Huan of Lu. (See note 112). A fish-trap is an image of a girl being married to a man. However, in this poem the fish-trap is a "broken" one, so that the fish in it "swims in and out" freely.

[116] This line is commonly read: "The lady from Qi goes to be married." But I follow Takata (382–3). See also the next song.

105. 載驅

105. Here Comes the Carriage

載驅薄薄
簟茀朱鞹
魯道有蕩
齊子發夕

Here comes the carriage running *bao bao*,
Bamboo awning, red leatherwork.
Broad is the Lu road,
The lady from Qi[117] has left at dusk.

四驪濟濟
垂轡濔濔
魯道有蕩
齊子豈弟

The four black steeds beautiful,
The reins dangling freely.
Broad is the Lu road,
The lady from Qi is in good humor.

汶水湯湯
行人彭彭
魯道有蕩
齊子翱翔

The waters of the Wen[118] are in full flood.
Travelers many on the road,
Broad is the Lu road,
The lady from Qi is buoyant.

汶水滔滔
行人儦儦
魯道有蕩
齊子游遨

The waters of the Wen are rapid.
Passersby ceaseless on the road,
Broad is the Lu road,
The lady from Qi is on a joyful journey.

---

[117] Wen Jiang, the wife of Duke Huan of Lu. The song is traditionally read in view of Wen Jiang's incestuous relation with her brother, Duke Rang of Qi. She is on her trip back home to Qi.

[118] The Wen is the river that runs between the states of Lu (to the south) and Qi (to the north).

106. 猗嗟

106. Ah, How Splendid!

猗嗟昌兮
頎而長兮
抑若揚兮
美目揚兮
巧趨蹌兮
射則臧兮

Ah, how splendid he is!
Tall and magnificent!
How noble his forehead!
How beautiful his eyes!
How light his quick steps!
How well he shoots!

猗嗟名兮
美目清兮
儀既成兮
終日射侯
不出正兮
展我甥兮

Ah, how remarkable he is!
His beautiful eyes so clear!
His manners perfect!
He may shoot all day,
Never missing the target.
Indeed, he is my nephew.

猗嗟孌兮
清揚婉兮
舞則選兮
射則貫兮
四矢反兮
以禦亂兮

Ah, how adorable he is!
Lovely are his clean eyebrows.
In dance, how he stands out!
In archery, how he hits the bull's eye,
All four arrows, one after another.[119]
A man who may quell any disorder.

---

[119] In an archery contest, a set of four arrows is used.

IX. 魏風 Wei Feng[120]

---

[120] For this chapter title see note 15 on the title of Chap. V. This state of Wei was located in the southern part of the present Shanxi province, where the Yellow River, coming down from the north, makes a big bend to begin to flow east. This region was known for the extreme frugality of its people, especially its ruling classes, which the very first poem in this chapter is usually read to allude to.

107. 葛屨

糾糾葛屨
可以履霜
摻摻女手
可以縫裳
要之襋之
好人服之

好人提提
宛然左辟
佩其象揥
維是褊心
是以為刺

107. Cloth-shoes

Cloth-shoes, so tightly woven,
Enable you to walk on the frost.
A girl's hands, so slender,
Can sew clothes,
The waist, the neck,
For a nobleman to wear.

The nobleman, correct in conduct,
Quietly, steps aside to the left.
An ivory comb at his belt.
Yet his niggardly mind
I fault him for that.

108. 汾沮洳

彼汾沮洳
言采其莫
彼其之子
美無度
美無度
殊異乎公路

彼汾一方
言采其桑
彼其之子
美如英
美如英
殊異乎公行

彼汾一曲
言采其藚
彼其之子
美如玉
美如玉
殊異乎公族

108. In That Wetland of the Fen

In that wetland of the Fen
I was plucking the sorrel.
That young man came by,
Handsome beyond words,
Handsome beyond words,
How striking at the duke's procession.

On that shore of the Fen
I was picking the mulberry leaves.
That young man came by,
Handsome as a flower,
Handsome as a flower.
How striking among the duke's entourage.

By that bend of the Fen
I was plucking the horsetail.
That young man came by,
Handsome as jade,
Handsome as jade,
How striking among the duke's clan.

109. 園有桃

109. In the Garden Is a Peach Tree

園有桃	In the garden is a peach tree,
其實之殽	Its fruits are our food.
心之憂矣	My worries
我歌且謠	Make me sing and chant.
不我知者	One who doesn't know me
謂我士也驕	Says "You are an impudent fellow."
彼人是哉	Is he right?
子曰何其	What do you say?
心之憂矣	My worries,[121]
其誰知之	Who knows them?
其誰知之	Who knows them?
蓋亦勿思	Better quit thinking of them.
園有棘	In the garden is a jujube tree,
其實之食	Its fruits are our food.
心之憂矣	My worries
聊以行國	Make me wander from place to place.
不我知者	One who doesn't know me
謂我士也罔極	Says "You are an imsolent fellow."
彼人是哉	Is he right?
子曰何其	What do you say?
心之憂矣	My worries,
其誰知之	Who knows them?
其誰知之	Who knows them?
蓋亦勿思	Better quit thinking of them.

---

[121] What worries? The song doesn't tell us. But commentators generally interpret this as a song lamenting the political or economic condition of the state.

110. 陟岵

陟彼岵兮　　　　　I climb that wooded hill,
瞻望父兮　　　　　I look toward where my father is.
父曰嗟予子　　　　My father says, Ah, son,
行役夙夜無已　　　You will be on duty day and night, without a break.

上慎旃哉　　　　　I pray, be careful,
猶來無止　　　　　Come back home, don't die.

陟彼屺兮　　　　　I climb that bare hill,
瞻望母兮　　　　　I look toward where my mother is.
母曰嗟予季　　　　My mother says, Ah, son,
行役夙夜無寐　　　You will be on duty day and night, without sleep.

上慎旃哉　　　　　I pray, be careful,
猶來無棄　　　　　Come back home, don't get killed.

陟彼岡兮　　　　　I climb that hill top,
瞻望兄兮　　　　　I look toward where my brother is.
兄曰嗟予弟　　　　My brother says, Ah, brother,
行役夙夜必偕　　　You will be on duty day and night, but never be alone.

上慎旃哉　　　　　I pray, be careful,
猶來無死　　　　　Come back home, don't die.

111. 十畝之間　　111. Ten-acre Field

十畝之間兮　　In the ten-acre field,
桑者閑閑兮　　The mulberry pickers are enjoying their
　　　　　　　　break.
行與子還兮　　Come, let's go.

十畝之外兮　　Beyond the ten-acre field,
桑者泄泄兮　　The mulberry pickers are cooling it.
行與子逝兮　　Come, let's go.

112. 伐檀

坎坎伐檀兮
寘之河之干兮
河水清且漣猗
不稼不穡
胡取禾三百廛兮

不狩不獵
胡瞻爾庭有縣貆兮

彼君子兮
不素餐兮

坎坎伐輻兮
寘之河之側兮
河水清且直猗
不稼不穡
胡取禾三百億兮

不狩不獵
胡瞻爾庭有縣特兮

彼君子兮
不素食兮

112. Cut the *Tan* Tree

Kan kan, cut the *tan*[122] tree,
Lay it on the river bank.
The waters are clear, rippling.
Without sowing, without reaping,
How do you get three hundred stacks of
    grain crops?
Without chasing, without hunting,
How can you see those badgers hanging
    in your courtyard?
Ah, that gentleman
Doesn't live on plain meal.[123]

Kan kan, cut the spokes,
Lay it on the riverside.
The waters are clear, ruffled.
Without sowing, without reaping,
How do you get three hundred million
    grains?
Without chasing, without hunting,
How can you see those adult animals
    hanging in your courtyard?
Ah, that gentleman
Doesn't live on plain meal.

---

[122] A large hardwood tree, from which cart wheels were made. Hard to identify it today.

[123] The key word in this line is *sucan*. In its idiomatic usage, to live on *sucan* means to live without working. But Shirakawa reads *sucan* in its literal sense, that is, in the sense of simple, plain meal (334).

坎坎伐輪兮
寘之河之漘兮
河水清且淪猗
不稼不穡
胡取禾三百囷兮

不狩不獵
胡瞻爾庭有縣鶉兮

彼君子兮
不素飧兮

Kan kan, cut the wheels,
Lay it on the river bank.
The waters are clear, churning up.
Without sowing, without reaping,
How do you get three hundred bins of
    grain?
Without chasing, without hunting,
How can you see those quails hanging in
    your courtyard?
Ah, that gentleman
Doesn't live on plain meal.

113. 碩鼠

碩鼠碩鼠
無食我黍
三歲貫女
莫我肯顧
逝將去女
適彼樂土
樂土樂土
爰得我所

碩鼠碩鼠
無食我麥
三歲貫女
莫我肯德
逝將去女
適彼樂國
樂國樂國
爰得我直

碩鼠碩鼠
無食我苗
三歲貫女
莫我肯勞

逝將去女
適彼樂郊
樂郊樂郊
誰之永號

113. Big Rat

Big rat, big rat!
Don't eat our millet!
For three years we have labored for you,
Yet you have never looked at us.
At last we are going to leave you
For that joyful land.
Joyful land, joyful land!
Where we will have our place.

Big rat, big rat!
Don't eat our wheat!
For three years we have labored for you,
Yet you have never shown us generosity.
At last we are going to leave you
For that joyful kingdom.
Joyful kingdom, joyful kingdom!
Where we will have our due.

Big rat, big rat!
Don't eat our rice seedlings.
For three years we have labored for you,
Yet you have never recognized our
   hardship.
At last we are going to leave you
For that joyful country.
Joyful country, joyful country!
Where no laments are sung.

X. 唐風　Tang Feng[124]

---

[124] This chapter contains songs from the state of Jin, one of the larger states of the Zhou kingdom. The chapter title comes from the former name of this region, Tang, which occupied the north-central part of the kingdom; covering the good part of the present Shanxi province.

x

X. 唐風　Tang Feng[124]

---

114. 蟋蟀

114. Crickets

蟋蟀在堂
歲聿其莫
今我不樂
日月其除
無已大康
職思其居
好樂無荒
良士瞿瞿

Crickets are in the house,
The year is soon coming to an end.
If we don't enjoy ourselves now,
The days and months will pass away.
Don't go overboard merry-making,
You ought to think of your homestead.
Enjoy yourself, but don't go wild,
A good man always stays within bounds.

蟋蟀在堂
歲聿其逝
今我不樂
日月其邁
無已大康
職思其外
好樂無荒
良士蹶蹶

Crickets are in the house,
The year is soon over.
If we don't enjoy ourselves now,
The days and months will go away.
Don't go overboard merry-making,
You ought to think of your work outside.
Enjoy yourself, but don't go wild,
A good man never forgets his work.

蟋蟀在堂
役車其休
今我不樂
日月其慆
無已大康
職思其憂
好樂無荒
良士休休

Crickets are in the house,
The field-wagons are at rest.
If we don't enjoy ourselves now,
The days and months will be gone wasted.
Don't go overboard merry-making,
You ought to think of worrisome things.
Enjoy yourself, but don't go wild,
A good man always behaves with
    moderation.

115. 山有樞

115. In the Mountain Grows the Thorn-elm

山有樞	In the mountain grows the thorn-elm,
隰有榆	In the lowland grows the white elm.
子有衣裳	You have long robes,
弗曳弗婁	Yet neither wear nor drag them.
子有車馬	You have carriages and horses,
弗馳弗驅	Yet neither gallop nor drive them.
宛其死矣	When you are dead and gone,
他人是愉	Someone else will enjoy them.
山有栲	In the mountain grows the green chinquapin,
隰有杻	In the lowland grows the privet.
子有廷內	You have courtyard and house,
弗洒弗埽	Yet neither sprinkle nor sweep them.
子有鐘鼓	You have bells and drums,
弗鼓弗考	Yet neither beat nor pound them.
宛其死矣	When you are dead and gone,
他人是保	Someone else will treasure them.
山有漆	In the mountain grows the lacquer-tree,
隰有栗	In the lowland grows the chestnut.
子有酒食	You have wine and fine food,
何不日鼓瑟	Yet never pluck your zither.
且以喜樂	Why don't you amuse yourself
且以永日	And make your days longer?
宛其死矣	When you are dead and gone,
他人入室	Someone else will enter your house.

116. 揚之水

116. Spraying Stream[125]

揚之水
白石鑿鑿
素衣朱襮
從子于沃
既見君子
云何不樂

The spraying stream,
The white stones shine *zao zao*.
Your white robe, red jacket,
I will accompany you to Wo.
Seeing you,
How wouldn't I be happy?

揚之水
白石皓皓
素衣朱繡
從子于鵠
既見君子
云何其憂

The spraying stream,
The white stones shine *hao hao*.
Your white robe, red embroidery,
I will accompany you to Gu.
Seeing you,
How would I be worried?

揚之水
白石粼粼
我聞有命
不敢以告人

The spraying stream,
The white stones shine *lin lin*.
I have heard your loving words,[126]
I won't tell anyone.

---

[125] The same title has already appeared twice (Nos. 68, 92) before. As indicated in note 96, I read the lines referring to "the spraying stream" as a reading of divination by water flow. In the earlier songs, the omen from the divination was bad, since "the bundle of firewood" (or its variants) was *not carried off* by the stream. In the present case, "the white stones" shine brilliantly, which may be taken as an indication of a good omen—that is, the bundle used was *carried away*, without being caught by the stones.

[126] Shirakawa's reading (349).

117. 椒聊

椒聊之實
蕃衍盈升
彼其之子
碩大無朋
椒聊且
遠條且

椒聊之實
蕃衍盈匊
彼其之子
碩大且篤
椒聊且
遠條且

117. Pepper-plant

That luxuriant pepper-plant,
Its seeds will fill the pint-measure.
That man,
Tall and strong, beyond match!
Oh, the pepper-plant,
How long its branches spread!

That luxuriant pepper-plant,
Its seeds will fill the cupped two hands.
That man,
Tall and strong, also kind!
Oh, that pepper-plant,
How long its branches spread!

118. 綢繆

118. Firewood Fast Bundled

綢繆束薪	The firewood fast bundled,[127]
三星在天	The Three Stars[128] are up in the sky.
今夕何夕	Tonight, what a night!
見此良人	Here this fine man is with me.
子兮子兮	Ah, ah!
如此良人何	What am I to do with this fine man?

綢繆束芻	The hay fast bundled,
三星在隅	The Three Stars are at the corner.
今夕何夕	Tonight, what a night!
見此邂逅	Here we enjoy our joyous union.[129]
子兮子兮	Ah, ah!
如此邂逅何	What am I to do with this joyous union?

綢繆束楚	The brushwood fast bundled,
三星在戶	The Three Stars are at the door.
今夕何夕	Tonight, what a night!
見此粲者	Here this beautiful man is with me.
子兮子兮	Ah, ah!
如此粲者何	What am I to do with this beautiful man?

---

[127] "The firewood fast bundled" (also the similar first lines in these other verses of the song) stands for marriage. Accordingly, this song is commonly read as the excitement and joy at the wedding night. I have read *liang ren* in the first verse as "good man" and *can zhe* in the last verse as "beautiful man," only because no gender-free expressions in English would sound quite natural. But Takata may be right in noting that the two Chinese words are used here gender-free (see Takata, 432). In this case, the song may be sung not only by the bridegroom but also by both the bride and bridegroom together.

[128] Orion's Belt.

[129] The basic meaning of the compound word *xiehou* is "chance-meeting." However, Takata points out that the character *xie* could also mean "joyful" (Takata, 432).

119. 杕杜

119. Lone Wild Pear-tree[130]

有杕之杜　　　There stands a lone wild pear-tree,
其葉湑湑　　　Its leaves dense.
獨行踽踽　　　Alone I am on the road, trudging along.
豈無他人　　　Not that there are no other people,
不如我同父　　None is like your own siblings.
嗟行之人　　　Ah, traveler,
胡不比焉　　　Why don't you befriend me?
人無兄弟　　　Here is a person without brothers,
胡不佽焉　　　Why don't you help me?

有杕之杜　　　There stands a lone wild pear-tree,
其葉菁菁　　　Its leaves lush.
獨行睘睘　　　Alone I am on the road, forlorn,
豈無他人　　　Not that there are no other people.
不如我同姓　　None is like your own siblings.
嗟行之人　　　Ah, traveler,
胡不比焉　　　Why don't you befriend me?
人無兄弟　　　Here is a person without brothers,
胡不佽焉　　　Why don't you help me?

---

[130] Sirakawa reads this song as a lonely woman's entreating of favor from passers-by (354). But this seems unnecessary. See another song with a similar title below (No. 123).

120. 羔裘

羔裘豹袪
自我人居居
豈無他人
維子之故

羔裘豹褎
自我人究究
豈無他人
維子之好

120. Lamb Coat

In your lamb coat, leopard fur sleeves,
You treat us so haughtily.
Are there no other lords?
We serve you only for old time's sake.

In your lamb coat, leopard fur sleeves,
You treat us so harshly.
Are there no other lords?
We serve you only because of our love
for you.

121. 鴇羽

蕭蕭鴇羽
集于苞栩
王事靡盬
不能蓺稷黍
父母何怙
悠悠蒼天
曷其有所

蕭蕭鴇翼
集于苞棘
王事靡盬
不能蓺黍稷
父母何食
悠悠蒼天
曷其有極

蕭蕭鴇行
集于苞桑
王事靡盬
不能蓺稻梁
父母何嘗
悠悠蒼天
曷其有常

121. Bustards in the Sky

Su Su, the bustards in the sky,
They come down on the oak clump.
The king's work never ceasing,
We cannot plant the millet.
Whom can our parents rely on?
Oh, the blue sky so far away!
When will we be home?

Su Su, the bustards, flying,
They come down on the thorn-bushes.
The king's work never ceasing.
We cannot plant the millet.
What will our parents eat?
Oh, the blue sky so far away!
When will all this come to an end?

Su Su, the bustards in the sky,
They come down on the mulberry field.
The king's work never ceasing.
We cannot plant the rice.
What can our parents relish?
Oh, the blue sky so far away!
When will we have our days in peace?

122. 無衣

豈曰無衣七兮

不如子之衣
安且吉兮

豈曰無衣六兮

不如子之衣
安且燠兮

122. I Have No Clothes

Why I say I have no clothes when I have
  seven?
None is like yours,
So comfortable and fine.

Why I say I have no clothes when I have
  six?
None is like yours,
So comfortable and warm.

123. 有杕之杜

有杕之杜
生于道左
彼君子兮
噬肯適我
中心好之
曷飲食之

有杕之杜
生于道周
彼君子兮
噬肯來游
中心好之
曷飲食之

123. There Grows a Lone Wild Pear-tree

There grows a lone wild pear-tree
On the left side of the road.
Ah, that gentleman,
I wish he would come to me.
From my heart I love him.
What dish would I offer him?

There grows a lone wild pear-tree
At that bend of the road.
Ah, that gentleman,
I wish he would visit me.
From my heart I love him.
What drink would I offer him?

124. 葛生

葛生蒙楚
蘞蔓于野
予美亡此
誰與獨處

葛生蒙棘

蘞蔓于域
予美亡此
誰與獨息

角枕粲兮
錦衾爛兮
予美亡此
誰與獨旦

夏之日
冬之夜
百歲之後
歸於其居

冬之夜
夏之日
百歲之後
歸於其室

124. The Cloth-plant Grows

The cloth-plant grows over the brambles,
The bindweed spreads over the field.
My beloved is here no more.
With whom? Alone I am left behind.

The cloth-plant grows over the thorn-
        bushes,
The bindweed spreads to the graveside.
My beloved is here no more.
With whom? Alone I lie in bed.

How beautiful the horn pillow,
How brilliant the embroidered coverlet!
My beloved is here no more.
With whom? Alone I stay awake till dawn.

Summer days,
Winter nights,
A hundred years from now,
I shall go where he dwells.

Winter nights,
Summer days,
A hundred years from now,
I shall go to his chamber.

125. 采苓

采苓采苓
首陽之巔
人之為言
苟亦無信
舍旃舍旃
苟亦無然
人之為言
胡得焉

采苦采苦
首陽之下
人之為言
苟亦無與
舍旃舍旃
苟亦無然
人之為言
胡得焉

采葑采葑
首陽之東
人之無言
苟亦無從
舍旃舍旃
苟亦無然
人之為言
胡得焉

125. Gather Licorice

We gather licorice, gather licorice
At the hilltop of Shouyang.
What people tell,
Don't believe it.
Ignore it, ignore it.
It's not true.
What people say,
What good comes of it?

We gather sow-thistle, gather sow-thistle
At the foot of Shouyang.
What people tell,
Don't heed it.
Ignore it, ignore it.
It's not true.
What people say,
What good comes of it?

We gather turnip, gather turnip
At the east of Shouyang.
What people tell,
Don't follow it.
Ignore it, ignore it.
It's not true.
What people say,
What good comes of it?

XI. 秦風 Qin Feng[131]

---

[131] The state of Qin, rising originally in the westernmost region of ancient China, gradually established itself in the present Shaanxi province, esp. after the move of the Zhou capital to the east, Loyang (717 BCE). The songs included in Qin Feng are believed to have come mostly from the region during the early years of the Eastern Zhou.

126. 車鄰

有車鄰鄰
有馬白顛
未見君子
寺人之令

阪有漆
隰有栗
既見君子
並坐鼓瑟
今者不樂
逝者其耋

阪有桑
隰有楊
既見君子
並坐鼓簧
今者不樂
逝者其亡

126. The Carriage Rolling

The carriage coming *lin lin*,
The horse, white hair on its forehead.
I don't see my lord yet,
His herald announces his coming.

On the hill grows the lacquer-tree,
On the lowland the chestnut-tree.
I now see my lord,
We sit side by side, he plucks the zither.
If you don't make merry today,
Soon you will be old.

On the hill grows the mulberry-tree,
On the lowland the poplar-tree.
I now see my lord,
We sit side by side, he plays the *huang*. [132]
If you don't make merry today,
Soon you will be gone.

---

[132] See note 95.

127. 駟驖

駟驖孔阜
六轡在手
公之媚子
從公于狩

奉時辰牡
辰牡孔碩
公曰左之
舍拔則獲

遊于北園
四馬既閑
輶車鸞鑣

載獫歇驕

127. Four Black Horses

His team of four black horses stout,
The six reins in his hand,
The duke's favorite son
Is hunting, following the duke.

On the run is a stag,
A huge stag of the season.
"To the left," says the duke.
He lets the arrow fly, makes his hit.

Coming to the north park,
The four horses are resting.
There goes the light wagon, bridle bells
    ringing,
The hunting dogs inside.

128. 小戎　　　128. Small War-chariot

小戎俴收　　　The small war-chariot, its low railings,
五楘梁輈　　　The five leather bands wrapped around its
　　　　　　　　　chariot-bar,
游環脅驅　　　The slip rings on the horses, the leather checks
　　　　　　　　　on the inside horses,
陰靷鋈續　　　The traces lodged by silver rings on the front board,
文茵暢轂　　　The mat of tiger hide on it, and the long naves
　　　　　　　　　under,
駕我騏馵　　　The chariot drawn by our piebalds and white-foots.[133]
言念君子　　　Ah, I think of my dear man,
溫其如玉　　　He was fair-minded as jade.
在其板屋　　　Now he lies in state in a plank hut,
亂我心曲　　　This roils my heart.

四牡孔阜　　　His four steeds are strong,
六轡在手　　　Six reins held in hands,
騏駵是中　　　The red horse and the white-footed one inside,
騧驪是驂　　　The brown horse and the black one outside,
龍盾之合　　　The dragon shields joined,
鋈以觼軜　　　The inner reins with silvered buckles.
言念君子　　　Ah, I think of my dear man,
溫其在邑　　　He lies in peace in that village.
方何為期　　　When shall we meet again?
胡然我念之　　How can I keep thinking like this?

---

[133] In these lines one reads a detailed listing of many parts of this war-chariot, often without indicating the relation of the parts mentioned, which makes it all but impossible for the modern reader to follow the description intelligently. In translating this poem, I have followed Takata's account of the chariot and its horses (Takata, 455–458). Still, my translation is tentative.

俴駟孔群
厹矛鋈錞
蒙伐有苑
虎韔鏤膺

交韔二弓
竹閉緄縢
言念君子
載寢載興
厭厭良人
秩秩德音

The light armored horses, well trained,
The tridents with silvered butts,
The colorful shields,
The tiger-skin quivers, the martingales metal inlaid.
The two bows, stretched across each other,
Are lashed to a bamboo case with rattan rope.
Ah, I think of my dear man,
In bed, out of bed.
How tender was this good man!
How gentle his voice!

129. 蒹葭

蒹葭蒼蒼
白露為霜
所謂伊人
在水一方
溯洄從之
道阻且長
溯游從之
宛在水中央

蒹葭淒淒
白露未晞
所謂伊人
在水之湄
溯洄從之
道阻且躋
溯游從之
宛在水中坻

蒹葭采采
白露未已
所謂伊人
在水之涘
溯洄從之
道阻且右
溯游從之
宛在水中沚

129. Rush[134]

The rush leaves so blue,
The white dew turns to frost.
This lady of my dream
Appears on the far side of the river.
I row upstream, following her,
The way is rough and far.
I row downstream, following her,
It's as though she is in the middle of the water.

The rush leaves so blue,
The white dew isn't dried yet.
This lady of my dream
Appears on the water's edge.
I row upstream, following her,
The way is rough and steep.
I row downstream, following her,
It's as though she is on the isle.

The rush leaves so desolate,
The white dew still remaining.
This lady of my dream
Appears near the shore.
I go upstream, following her,
The way is rough, turns right.
I go downstream, following her,
It's as though she is on the shoals.

---

[134] Shirakawa reads this as a song of the goddess of the river (381–382, see also her *Shi Kyō*, 51–53).

130. 終南

終南何有
有條有梅
君子至止
錦衣狐裘
顏如渥丹
其君也哉

終南何有
有紀有堂
君子至止
黻衣繡裳

佩玉將將
壽考不忘

130. Zhongnan

What grows on Mt. Zhongnan?
Peach-trees and plum-trees.[135]
My lord has arrived.
The brocaded robe over the fur coat,
His face rosy as if rouged.
Indeed he is my lord!

What is on Mt. Zhongnan?
The boxthorn and the wild pear.
My lord has arrived.
His robe brocaded in black and blue, the
  skirt embroidered.
His girdle jades tinkling.
Long may he live in peace.

---

[135] The two plant names in this line, *tiao* and *mei*, are hard to identify in English; I translate them here only tentatively, following Waley. On the basis of several commentaries, I believe the two characters meant something other than what they now usually mean.

131. 黃鳥

交交黃鳥
止于棘
誰從穆公
子車奄息
維此奄息
百夫之特
臨其穴
惴惴其慄
彼蒼者天
殲我良人
如可贖兮
人百其身

交交黃鳥
止于桑
誰從穆公
子車仲行
維此仲行
百夫之防
臨其穴
惴惴其慄
彼蒼者天
殲我良人
如可贖兮
人百其身

131. Oriole

Jie jie sings the oriole,
Perching on the thorn-bush.
Who follows Duke Mu to the grave?[136]
Yanxi of Ziche,
This Yanxi
Is the best of our hundred men.
Looking into the grave-pit,
He trembles from fear.
Oh, that blue one, Heaven,
Is killing our good man.
Were it possible to redeem him by dying,
A hundred would give their lives.

Jie jie sings the oriole,
Perching on the mulberry tree.
Who follows Duke Mu to the grave?
Zhonghang of Ziche,
This Zhonghang
Can fend off a hundred enemies.
Looking into the grave-pit,
He trembles from fear.
Oh, that blue one, Heaven,
Is killing our good man.
Were it possible to redeem him by dying,
A hundred would give their lives.

---

[136] Duke Mu of Qin died in 621 BCE. Following to him to the grave were three sons of *Ziche*: Yanxi, Zhonghang, and Zhenhu.

交交黃鳥　　　　*Jie jie* sings the oriole,
止于楚　　　　　Perching on the bramble-bush.
誰從穆公　　　　Who follows Duke Mu to the grave?
子車鍼虎　　　　Zhenhu of Ziche,
維此鍼虎　　　　This Zhenhu
百夫之禦　　　　Can ward off a hundred enemies.
臨其穴　　　　　Looking into the grave-pit,
惴惴其慄　　　　He trembles from fear.
彼蒼者天　　　　Oh, that blue one, Heaven,
殲我良人　　　　Is killing our good man.
如可贖兮　　　　Were it possible to redeem him by dying,
人百其身　　　　A hundred would give their lives.

132. 晨風

歇彼晨風
鬱彼北林
未見君子
憂心欽欽
如何如何
忘我實多

山有苞櫟
隰有六駮
未見君子
憂心靡樂
如何如何
忘我實多

山有苞棣
隰有樹檖
未見君子
憂心如醉
如何如何
忘我實多

132. Morning Wind[137]

How gusty the morning wind,
How dense the north wood!
Not seeing you,
My grieving heart is in deep despair.
Why, why?
You forget me so often.

On the hill grows the buckeye shrub,
On the lowland grows the spindle-tree.
Not seeing you,
My grieving heart is joyless,
Why, why?
You forget me so often.

On the hill grows the plum-tree,
On the lowland grows the pear-tree.
Not seeing you,
My heart is drunk on grief.
Why, why?
You forget me so often.

---

[137] In this poem, *chen feng* is usually translated as "falcon." However, I follow Takata (469).

133. 無衣

岂曰無衣
與子同袍
王于興師
修我戈矛
與子同仇

岂曰無衣
與子同澤
王于興師
修我矛戟
與子偕作

岂曰無衣
與子同裳
王于興師
修我甲兵
與子偕行

133. No Clothes

Why do you say you have no clothes?
With you I will share my jacket.
When the king raises an army,
We will have our spears ready.
With you I will fight our enemy.

Why do you say you have no clothes?
With you I will share my underclothes.
When the king raises an army,
We will have our tridents ready.
With you I will go to war together.

Why do you say you have no clothes?
With you I will share my skirt.
When the king raises an army,
We will have our weapons ready.
With you I will go to the battlefield
    together.

134. 渭陽

我送舅氏
曰至渭陽
何以贈之
路車乘黃

我送舅氏
悠悠我思
何以贈之
瓊瑰玉佩

134. The North of the Wei[138]

Escorting my uncle,
I reached the north of the Wei.
What present did I give him?
A chariot with a team of bays.

Escorting my uncle,
My thoughts were endless.
What present did I give him?
A girdle studded with gems.

---

[138] This is generally understood as a poem by Duke Kang of Qin. During the time when his father, Duke Mu, was still living, his maternal uncle, Zhong'er, came to stay in Qin, escaping from the rebellion in the neighboring state, Jin. After the restoration of the peace in Jin, Zhong'er returns to his state, escorted by his nephew, the future Duke Kang, as far as the north of the Wei.

135. 權輿

於我乎
夏屋渠渠

今也每食無餘

于嗟乎
不承權輿

於我乎
每食四簋
今也每食不飽
于嗟乎
不承權輿

135. Gone Are the Flourishing Days

Ah, our life!
We used to have our dish-stands towering
high.
Now, we leave nothing on the dish at the
table.
Ah!
Our flourishing days are long gone.

Ah, our life!
We used to have four dishes at each meal,
Now, we never eat enough.
Ah!
Our flourishing days are long gone.

XII. 陳風 Chen Feng[139]

---

[139] The state of Chen occupied the southeastern part of the present Henan province. Included in this chapter are ten songs, which are mostly related to dance festivals (Shirakawa, 339). This fact is generally explained in view of the popular tradition of shaman dance in the state, which originated from the time of its founding.

136. 宛丘

子之湯兮
宛丘之上兮
洵有情兮
而無望兮

坎其擊鼓
宛丘之下
無冬無夏
值其鷺羽

坎其擊缶
宛丘之道
無冬無夏
值其鷺翿

136. Wanqiu

How resplendent everybody is
On the hilltop of Wanqiu!
Truly a delightful sight!
Never to forget.[140]

Kan kan, the drum beating
At the bottom of Wanqiu.
Be it winter, be it summer,
We all dance, waving egret feathers in our
    hands.

Kan kan, the vat beating
On the way up Wanqiu.
Be it winter, be it summer,
We all dance, waving egret feathers in our
    hands.

---

[140] Shirakawa's reading (401).

137. 東門之枌

東門之枌
宛丘之栩
子仲之子
婆娑其下

穀旦于差
南方之原
不績其麻
市也婆娑

穀旦于逝
越以鬷邁
視爾如荍
貽我握椒

137. Elms of the East Gate

The elms of the East Gate,
The oaks of Wanqiu.
The daughters of the Zizhong
Are dancing under the trees.

This chosen morning so gorgeous!
The Yuan daughters of the south side,
No longer spinning hemp,
Are dancing in the market.

Let's go, this beautiful morning!
Join the crowd!
"You look as lovely as the hollyhock,
You gave me a handful of pepper seeds.[141]"

---

[141] Women give pepper seeds as a token of love.

138. 衡門

衡門之下
可以棲遲
泌之洋洋
可以樂飢

豈其食魚
必河之魴

豈其取妻
必齊之姜

豈其食魚
必河之鯉

豈其取妻
必宋之子

138. Single-bar Gate[142]

Under that single-bar gate
Let us hide together.
By the flowing spring
Let us satisfy our thirst.

The fish to eat,
Why must it be bream from the Yellow
River?
The girl to marry,
Why must she be from the Jiang of Qi[143]?

The fish to eat,
Why must it be carp from the Yellow
River?
The girl to marry,
Why must she be from the Ji of Song[144]?

---

[142] I read this as a song of love-making, following Shirakawa's interpretation (403–5, see also Mekada, 100). In this reading, e.g., in the first verse, "thirst" may be taken to mean sexual desire. Shirakawa especially notes that "fish" in ancient China was commonly used as a figurative reference to a woman (see 405 and Shirakawa, *Shi Kyō*, .42).

[143] Jiang was the name of the ruling family of the state of Qi.

[144] Ji was the name of the ruling family of the state of Song.

139. 東門之池

東門之池
可以漚麻
彼美淑姬
可與晤歌

東門之池
可以漚紵
彼美淑姬
可與晤語

東門之池
可以漚菅
彼美淑姬
可與晤言

139. The Pond by the East Gate

At the pond by the East Gate
You may steep hemp.
That beautiful maiden,
I like to sing with her.

At the pond by the East Gate
You may steep ramie.
That beautiful maiden,
I like to chat with her.

At the pond by the East Gate
You may steep sedge.
That beautiful maiden,
I like to talk to her.

140. 東門之楊

140. Willows of the East Gate

東門之楊
其葉牂牂
昏以為期
明星煌煌

The willows of the East Gate,
How lush their leaves!
At dusk we were to meet there,
But how bright is that morning star!

東門之楊
其葉肺肺
昏以為期
明星哲哲

The willows of the East Gate,
How dense their leaves!
At dusk we were to meet there,
But how twinkling is that morning star!

141. 墓門

墓門有棘
斧以斯之
夫也不良
國人知之
知而不已
誰昔然矣

墓門有梅
有鴞萃止
夫也不良
歌以訊之
訊予不顧
顛倒思予

141. The Cemetery Gate

By the cemetery gate grow thorn-bushes,
You cut them down with an ax.
That man is no good.
The people of this country know it.
But he won't quit.
For long he has been so.

By the cemetery gate stands a plum-tree,
Owls roost on it.
That man is no good.
Singing this song, I warn him.
But he won't heed me,
After his fall, he will think of me.

142. 防有鵲巢

142. On the Dyke

防有鵲巢
邛有旨苕
誰侜予美
心焉忉忉

On the dyke is a magpie's nest,
On the hill grows the sweet vetch.
Who is deceiving my beloved?
My heart is anxious.

中唐有甓

邛有旨鷊
誰侜予美
心焉惕惕

In the middle of the courtyard is a titled
    path,
On the hill grow colorful grasses.
Who is deceiving my beloved?
My heart is worried.

143. 月出

月出皎兮
佼人僚兮
舒窈糾兮
勞心悄兮

月出皓兮
佼人懰兮
舒懮受兮
勞心慅兮

月出照兮
佼人燎兮
舒夭紹兮
勞心慘兮

143. The Moon Rising[145]

How bright the moon rising!
My love so beautiful,
How graceful she is!
My forlorn heart pines.

How bright the moon rising!
My love so pretty,
How elegant she is!
My forlorn heart hurts.

How radiant the moon rising,
My love so bright,
How gracious she is!
My forlorn heart grieves.

---

[145] Shirakawa reads this as a song sung at a dance festival on a moonlit night (see 411–413).

144. 株林

胡為乎株林
從夏南
匪適株林
從夏南

駕我乘馬
說于株野
乘我乘駒
朝食于株

144. Zhulin[146]

How come you are heading for Zhulin?
We escort him to Xianan's.
Not to Zhulin,
But to Xianan's.

We ride our horse carriage,
Camp at the outskirts of Zhulin.
We ride our colt carriage,
Breakfast at Zhulin.

---

[146] This song refers to the scandalous visits of Duke Ling of Chen to Lady Xia
in Zhulin. Lady Xia, the widow of one of the duke's ministers, was known to
have several lovers simultaneously. Duke Ling was one of them. Xianan was her
son. "We" in the poem refers to the duke's escort. "Xianan's" is an indirect way
of referring to Xianan's mother, Lady Xia's place.

145. 澤陂

彼澤之陂
有蒲與荷
有美一人
傷如之何
寤寐無為
涕泗滂沱

彼澤之陂
有蒲與蕑
有美一人
碩大且卷
寤寐無為
中心悁悁

彼澤之陂
有蒲菡萏
有美一人
碩大且儼
寤寐無為
輾轉伏枕

145. Water's Edge

Along that water's edge
Grow reeds and lotuses.
There is a handsome man,
How he hurts my heart!
Asleep or awake, I can do nothing,
My tears streaming.

Along that water's edge
Grow reeds and fragrant grasses.
There is a handsome man,
Tall and elegant!
Asleep or awake, I can do nothing,
My heart in anguish.

Along that water's edge
Grow reeds and lotus-flowers.
There is a handsome man,
Tall and trim!
Asleep or awake, I can do nothing,
In bed, I toss and turn.

XIII. 檜風 Kuai Feng[147]

---

[147] Kuei was a tiny state adjacent to the state of Zheng, located to the northeast of the present Mi Xian of Henan Province. Soon after the Zhou court's move to the east, Kuei was absorbed by Zheng.

146. 羔裘

羔裘逍遙
狐裘以朝
豈不爾思
勞心忉忉

羔裘翺翔
狐裘在堂
豈不爾思
我心憂傷

羔裘如膏
日出有曜
豈不爾思
中心是悼

146. Lamb Coat

In your lamb coat you stroll,
In your fox coat you attend court.
How can I help thinking of you?
My heart is in anguish.

In your lamb coat you solemnly walk,
In your fox coat you sit in the hall.
How can I help thinking of you?
My heart is in pain.

Your lamb coat so lustrous,
In the sun, your presence so brilliant.
How can I help thinking of you?
Inside, my heart grieves.

147. 素冠

庶見素冠兮

棘人欒欒兮
勞心慱慱兮

庶見素衣兮

我心傷悲兮
聊與子同歸兮

庶見素韠兮

我心蘊結兮
聊與子如一兮

147. White Cap[148]

Ah, I long to meet that man in a white cap!

Wistful, I am languishing.[149]
My anxious heart never eases.

Ah, I long to meet that man in a white coat!

My heart is grieving.
I wish I could accompany him home.

Ah, I long to meet that man in white leggings!

My heart is knotted.
I wish I could join him.

---

[148] This poem refers to a man in "white cap," "white coat," and "white leggings." According to the traditional Confucian ritual of mourning, these white items are to be worn by people in mourning. However, the poem antedates this ritual, possibly by two or more centuries. Therefore one may not necessarily interpret the "man" in these white items in this poem to be a man in mourning, the traditional Confucian interpretation of it notwithstanding. (See Shirakawa, 424, Mekata, 105).

[149] Sirakawa's reading (424).

148. 隰有萇楚

隰有萇楚
猗儺其枝
夭之沃沃
樂子之無知

隰有萇楚
猗儺其華
夭之沃沃
樂子之無家

隰有萇楚
猗儺其實
夭之沃沃
樂子之無室。

148. Brushwood in the Lowland

In the lowland grows the brushwood,
Delicate are its boughs.
How tender and fresh you are!
I am glad you are innocent.

In the lowland grows the brushwood,
Delicate are its flowers.
How tender and fresh you are!
I am glad you have no wife.

In the lowland grows the brushwood,
Delicate are its fruits.
How tender and fresh you are!
I am glad you have no family of your own.

149. 匪風

匪風發兮
匪車偈兮
顧瞻周道
中心怛兮

匪風飄兮
匪車嘌兮
顧瞻周道
中心弔兮

誰能亨魚
溉之釜鬵
誰將西歸
懷之好音

149. That Fierce Wind

Ah, that wind so fierce![150]
Ah, those war-wagons hustling!
I look back the Zhou highway.
Inside, my heart hurts.

Ah, that wind whirling!
Ah, those war-wagons rumbling!
I look back the Zhou highway.
Inside, my heart grieves.

Who can cook the fish?
I will wash the pot.
Who is returning to the west?
I will send home good words.

---

[150] In my reading of this and the next line, I follow Shriakawa and Mekada (427, Mekata, 106).

XIV. 曹風 Cao Feng[151]

---

[151] Cao was a small state between the states of Lu and Wei, situated in Caozhou of the present Shandong province.

150. 蜉蝣

蜉蝣之羽
衣裳楚楚
心之憂矣
於我歸處

蜉蝣之翼
采采衣服
心之憂矣
於我歸息

蜉蝣掘閱
麻衣如雪
心之憂矣
於我歸說

150. Mayfly[152]

The wings of the mayfly,
Your clothes so plain and pure.
My heart in sorrow,
I long to join you here.

The wings of the mayfly,
Your clothes so fine and pure.
My heart in sorrow,
I long to rest here with you.

The mayfly just out of its shell,
Your hemp clothes as pure as snow.
My heart in sorrow,
I long to stay here with you.

---

[152] Shirakawa reads this as a poem in which the surviving spouse grieves at the burial of the diseased one (see 434). I believe she is unique in this reading; however, I follow her reading, especially in view of the final verse, which refers to the hemp clothes of the dead.

151. 候人

彼候人兮
何戈與祋
彼其之子
三百赤芾

維鵜在梁
不濡其翼
彼其之子
不稱其服

維鵜在梁
不濡其咮
彼其之子
不遂其媾

薈兮蔚兮
南山朝隮
婉兮孌兮
季女斯飢

151. That Palace Guard

Ah, that man at arms!
He is bearing spear and staff.
That young man,
In that red uniform of the palace guards.

The pelican standing on the weir
Doesn't get its wings wet.
That young man
Doesn't merit his uniform.

The pelican standing on the weir
Doesn't get its beak wet.
That young man
Doesn't keep his tryst.

Oh, those dark clouds spreading over the
    south mountain,
There appears the morning rainbow.[153]
Oh, how beautiful! How lovely!
Those young girls are left in despair.

---

[153] See note 70.

152. 鳲鳩

152. Turtle-dove

鳲鳩在桑
其子七兮
淑人君子
其儀一兮
其儀一兮
心如結兮

The turtle-dove is on the mulberry-tree,
Its young are seven.
This noble lady and gentleman,[154]
Their good manners are one,
Their good manners are one,
Their minds as though bound.

鳲鳩在桑
其子在梅
淑人君子
其帶伊絲
其帶伊絲
其弁伊騏

The turtle-dove is on the mulberry-tree,
Its young are on the plum-tree.
This noble lady and gentleman,
Their girdles are white silk,
Their girdles are white silk,
Their caps are blue hide.

鳲鳩在桑
其子在棘
淑人君子
其儀不忒
其儀不忒
正是四國

The turtle-dove is on the mulberry-tree,
Its young are in the thorn-bush.
This noble lady and gentleman,
Their good manners are flawless,
Their good manners are flawless,
They will govern the land right.

鳲鳩在桑
其子在榛
淑人君子
正是國人
正是國人
胡不萬年

The turtle-dove is on the mulberry-tree,
Its young are on the hazel-tree.
This noble lady and gentleman,
May they lead the people right,
May they lead the people right,
For ten thousand years!

---

[154] Shirakawa's reading (441). She reads this song as a wedding song (441).

194

153. 下泉   153. How Cold that Spring

冽彼下泉
浸彼苞稂
愾我寤嘆
念彼周京

How cold that spring down there,
It soaks the clustering grass.
Wide awake, lamenting
I think of the Zhou capital.[155]

冽彼下泉
浸彼苞蕭
愾我寤嘆
念彼京周

How cold that spring down there,
It soaks the clustering sagebrush.
Wide awake, lamenting
I think of the capital of Zhou.

冽彼下泉
浸彼苞蓍
愾無寤嘆
念彼京師

How cold that spring down there,
It soaks the clustering yarrow.
Wide awake, lamenting
I think of the capital.

芃芃黍苗
陰雨膏之
四國有王
郇伯勞之

How vigorous those millet shoots!
Seasonal rain nourishes them.
All lands under the king,
The lord of Xun cared for the people.

---

[155] The song doesn't tell us exactly what "I think" of the capital, in this or in the next two verses. I take the final verse to be what is in the mind of the poet: the good, old days when the people were better off under the king's rule. The poet is "lamenting" because of the present hardship, which most commentators note. For instance, Shirakawa mentions heavy taxation as a probable reason for lamentation.

XV. 豳風 Bin Feng[156]

[156] Bin in this chapter title is not a state name of the Zhou dynasty. It is the name of the Zhou's old place of origin, situated in the northwestern part of the present Shaanxi province. Shirakawa believes that the songs included in this chapter came from this region most likely about the time of the Zhou's move to the east.

154. 七月

154. Seventh Month

七月流火	The seventh month,[157] the Fire[158] goes to the west,
九月授衣	The ninth month, we hand out the coats.
一之日觱發	The days of the First,[159] fierce wind,
二之日栗烈	The days of the Second, severe cold.
無衣無褐	Without coats, without woolen clothes,
何以卒歲	How are we to finish this year?
三之日于耜	The days of the Third,[160] we get our ploughs ready,
四之日舉趾	The days of the Fourth, we till.
同我婦子	With women and children
饁彼南畝	We eat lunch at the south acre,
田畯至喜	Farm officials gladly join us.
七月流火	The seventh month, the Fire goes to the west,
九月授衣	The ninth month, we hand out the coats.
春日載陽	Spring days get warmer,
有鳴倉庚	The oriole sings.
女執懿筐	The girls carry their deep baskets,

---

[157] This poem refers to two different lunar calendars, the Xia and the Zhou calendars. The numbered months such as "the seventh month" and "the ninth month" are of the former, and the ordinal numbers such as "the First," and "the Second" indicate the months of the latter. The Xia year began in the spring about two months after the Zhou year, which began at the time of the winter solstice—hence approximately a difference of two months. For instance, "the seventh month" in this line is of the Xia calendar, which is the ninth month of the Zhou calendar. This may sound somewhat confusing. However, one may see the seasons' progression through the year.

[158] A Chinese astronomical term, referring to Mars.

[159] "The First" (the first month of the Zhou calendar) is the eleventh month of the Xia calendar, and "the Second" in the next line the twelfth month of the Xia calendar.

[160] I.e., the first month of the Xia calendar (spring time).

遵彼微行	Along the narrow paths,
爰求柔桑	They gather soft mulberry-leaves.
春日遲遲	The spring days are splendid,
采蘩祁祁	They gather the white aster leisurely.
女心傷悲	Their hearts, lovelorn, sad,
殆及公子同歸	They wish to go with the young lord.
七月流火	The seventh month, the Fire goes to the west,
八月萑葦	The eighth month, we cut the rushes.
蠶月條桑	The silk-worm month, we pick mulberry-leaves
取彼斧斨	Grab those axes,
以伐遠揚	Lop the long branches,
猗彼女桑	Pull the tender mulberry-leaves.
七月鳴鵙	The seventh month, the shrike cries,
八月載績	The eighth month, we spin.
載玄載黃	Dye black, dye yellow,
我朱孔陽	My red is so bright,
為公子裳	I will make a robe for my young lord.
四月秀葽	The fourth month, the milkwort ripe,
五月鳴蜩	The fifth month, the cicada sings.
八月其穫	The eighth month, the harvest.
十月隕蘀	The tenth month, the leaves fall.
一之日于貉	The days of the First, we hunt the badger,
取彼狐狸	Catch foxes, wild cats,
為公子裘	To make a coat for our young lord.
二之日其同	The days of the Second, we all meet for hunting,
載纘武功	Also for our war practice.
言私其豵	This small boar for me,
獻豜于公	That large boar for my lord.
五月斯螽動股	The fifth month, the locust cries,
六月莎雞振羽	The sixth month, the grasshopper sings.
七月在野	The seventh month, it's out in the field,
八月在宇	The eighth month, under the eves,
九月在戶	The ninth month, at the door,

十月蟋蟀入我床下　The tenth month, the cricket is under
　　　　　　　　　　my bed.
穹室熏鼠　We stop up the gaps, smoke out the rats,
塞向墐戶　Plug the windows, paste the doors.
嗟我婦子　Ah, wife and children,
曰為改歲　The new year is approaching,
入此室處　Come indoors and stay.

六月食鬱及薁　The sixth month, we eat plums and wild
　　　　　　　　grapes,
七月亨葵及菽　The seventh month, cook mallows and
　　　　　　　　beans,
八月剝棗　The eighth month, beat the dates off the
　　　　　　branches.
十月穫稻　The tenth month, we harvest the rice,
為此春酒　Make spring wine with it,
以介眉壽　So that we may pray for a long life for
　　　　　　the old.
七月食瓜　The seventh month, we eat melons,
八月斷壺　The eighth month, cut the gourds,
九月叔苴　The ninth month, collect hemp seeds,
采荼薪樗　Pull bitter herbs and cut sumac for
　　　　　　firewood
食我農夫　For the upkeep of the farmers.

九月築場圃　The ninth month, we make the thrashing
　　　　　　　yard ready,
十月納禾稼　The tenth month, we store the harvest
　　　　　　　in the barn,
黍稷重穋　Millet, early rice, late rice,
禾麻菽麥　Hemp, beans, wheat.
嗟我農夫　Ah, our farmers,
我稼既同　Our harvesting is done.
上入執宮功　Now go in the house to work inside.
晝爾于茅　During the day, gather thatch-reeds,
宵爾索綯　At night, twist rope,
亟其乘屋　Before it's too late, get up on the roof to
　　　　　　repair.

其始播百穀	Soon you will begin to plant a hundred grains.
二之日鑿冰沖沖	The days of the Second, we cut the ice *zhong zhong*,
三之日納于凌陰	The days of the Third, we store it in the ice-room.
四之日其蚤	The days of the Fourth, in the early morning,
獻羔祭韭	We offer lamb and leek at the worship.
九月肅霜	The ninth month, heavy frost,
十月滌場	The tenth month, we clean the yard,
朋酒斯饗	Hold the feast with two barrels of wine.
曰殺羔羊	We kill a lamb,
躋彼公堂	Go in the lord's hall,
稱彼兕觥	Raise the wine-cups of buffalo horn,
萬壽無疆	Long live, our lord!

155. 鴟鴞

鴟鴞鴟鴞
既取我子
無毀我室
恩斯勤斯
鬻子之閔斯

迨天之未陰雨
徹彼桑土

綢繆牖戶
今女下民
或敢侮予

予手拮据
予所捋荼
予所蓄租
予口卒瘏
曰予未有室家

予羽譙譙
予尾翛翛
予室翹翹
風雨所漂搖
予維音嘵嘵

155. Owl[161]

Oh, owl, owl!
You have already taken my young,
Don't destroy my house.
Pity on this little one remaining,
I have reared it with such love and care.

Before the dark sky brings rain,
I am scratching the bark off the mulberry-
tree,
To fix the window and door.
You, people down below,
May not dare fault me.

My hands are all chafed,
I have collected reed ears,
Gathered straws for bedding.
My mouth all soar,
Still I have no house.

My wings ragged,
My tail draggled.
My house is about to fall apart,
Shaken by the wind and the rain.
I cry loud in despair.

---

[161] Traditionally this poem is read allegorically in light of the historical account (in the *Book of Documents*) of the incident in which the Duke of Zhou was falsely accused of trying to usurp the throne from the young King Cheng. The *Mao Xu* attributes its authorship to the Duke of Zhou himself. But such a reading is not necessary. See Shirakawa, 464 and Mekata, 114.

156. 東山

我徂東山
慆慆不歸
我來自東
零雨其濛
我東曰歸
我心西悲
制彼裳衣
勿士行枚
蜎蜎者蠋
烝在桑野
敦彼獨宿
亦在車下

我徂東山
慆慆不歸
我來自東
零雨其濛
果臝之實
亦施于宇
伊威在室
蠨蛸在戶
町畽鹿場
熠燿宵行
不可畏也
伊可懷也

156. Eastern Mountains

We went to the eastern mountains,[162]
For long I didn't return home.
Now I am back from the east,
It's drizzling and drizzling.
While in the east, longing to come home,
My mind was sad, thinking of the west.
Now, you have made me those clothes,
No more bamboo piece in my mouth.[163]
A wriggling silkworm
I was in the mulberry field for long.
All curled up I slept alone
Under that wagon.

We went to the eastern mountains,
For long I didn't return home.
Now I am back from the east,
It's drizzling and drizzling.
The fruit of that snake-gourd
Is reaching the eves,
Wood lice crawling in the rooms,
Spider webs on the door,
The field turning into a deer ground.
Witch fire flying at night,
All nothing to fear,
Rather, I missed them.

---

[162] On a military campaign.

[163] During the military campaign, a soldier was given a chopstick-like bamboo piece to keep in his mouth. This was to prevent him from groaning. See Takata, 551.

我祖東山
慆慆不歸
我來自東
零雨其濛
鸛鳴于垤
婦歎于室
洒掃穹窒
我征聿至
有敦瓜苦
烝在栗薪
自我不見
于今三年

我祖東山
慆慆不歸
我來自東
零雨其濛
倉庚于飛
熠燿其羽
之子于歸
皇駁其馬
親結其縭
九十其儀
其新孔嘉

其舊如之何

We went to the eastern mountains,
For long I didn't return home.
Now I am back from the east,
It's drizzling and drizzling.
A stork is crying on the anthill,
Wife, sighing in the house,
Washes, sweeps, closes the cracks,
At last I am back from the campaign.
Those bitter gourds, dangling,
Have spread over chestnut firewood.
I haven't seen them
Already for three years.

We went to the eastern mountains,
For long I didn't return home.
Now I am back from the east,
It's drizzling and drizzling.
An oriole in flight,
Its wings shining bright.
My wife on her way to our wedding,
Her horses, brown and yellow.
Her mother had tied her girdle strings,
How splendid was the ceremony!
How blissful was our matrimony then, so new!
How is it now, old?

157. 破斧

既破我斧
又缺我斨
周公東征
四國是皇

哀我人斯
亦孔之將

既破我斧
又缺我錡
周公東征
四國是吪

哀我人斯
亦孔之嘉

既破我斧
又缺我銶
周公東征
四國是遒

哀我人斯
亦孔之休

157. Broken Axes

Our axes were broken,
Our hatchets lost.
Since his eastern campaign,
The Duke of Zhou has brought order to the
    kingdom.
His compassion to us people
Is great indeed.

Our axes were broken,
Our chisels lost.
Since his eastern campaign,
The Duke of Zhou has transformed the
    kingdom.
His compassion to us people
Is such a blessing for us.

Our axes were broken,
Our hoes lost.
Since his eastern campaign,
The Duke of Zhou has brought unity to the
    kingdom.
His compassion to us people
Is such a comfort for us.

158. 伐柯

158. To Cut an Ax-handle

伐柯如何
匪斧不克
取妻如何
匪媒不得

How to cut an ax-handle?
Without an ax, you cannot make it.
How to take a wife?
Without a matchmaker, you cannot get her.

伐柯伐柯
其則不遠
我覯之子
籩豆有踐

Cut an ax-handle, cut an ax-handle!
The model is not far to seek.[164]
We see the bride and groom,
Here are the nuptial dishes in rows.[165]

---

[164] The model for an ax-handle to cut would be the very ax-handle being used for the cutting.

[165] Some commentators (e.g., Shirakawa) find the last two lines out of place. Why not read them simply as a description of a happy wedding scene, the result of a successful matchmaking?

159. 九罭

九罭之魚
鱒魴
我覯之子
袞衣繡裳

鴻飛遵渚
公歸無所
於女信處

鴻飛遵陸
公歸不復
於女信宿

是以有袞衣兮
無以我公歸兮
無使我心悲兮

159. Caught in the Small Net[166]

Caught in the small net
Is a large trout.
I see this man
In his dragon robe.

The large goose flies along the strand,
My lord, would you have no place to go?[167]
Please stay with us for a short while.

The large goose flies over the land,
My lord, once gone, you will never return,
Please stay over for a short while.

In your dragon robe,
Don't let them take you away, my lord.
Don't make my heart grieve.

---

[166] Zhu Xi reads this as a poem in which the people of the eastern part of the kingdom, where the Duke of Zhou had gone (see No. 157), implore him to stay longer before returning to the capital in the west. When so read, this song seems to make the best sense (see Mekata, 117).

[167] This particular line has been variously read. I follow Takata's reading (see Takata, 562).

160. 狼跋

狼跋其胡
載疐其尾
公孫碩膚
赤舄几几

狼疐其尾
載跋其胡
公孫碩膚
德音不瑕

160. The Wolf Stumbles[168]

The wolf stumbles on its own dewlap,
Trips on its own tail.[169]
My lord, tall and magnanimous,
Walks gravely in his red shoes.

The wolf trips on its own tail,
Stumbles on its own dewlap.
My lord, tall and magnanimous,
His glory will never fade.

---

[168] A poem in praise of the Duke of Zhou.

[169] One may question the pertinence of these lines regarding the stumbling and tripping wolf to the rest of the poem. But the lines may be read as a comical picture of a wicked, clumsy animal *in contrast* with the tall, gentle Duke of Zhou (see Takata, 564).

Appendix
Ren and the *Shi* in Confucius

1.

In the Introduction, I discussed how Confucius read the *Shi Jing*, citing a number of sayings from the *Analects*, in which he refers to the *Shi*.[1] His reading of the *Shi* was essentially aesthetic. I stressed this point in order to show how this was different from the traditional Confucian reading of the *Shi Jing*. In this essay, I will discuss his aesthetic reading of the *Shi*, especially in view of his teaching of *ren*.

Perhaps few would question the centrality of *ren* in Confucius's teachings. The character *ren* is variously translated in English, commonly as "humanity," "human-heartedness," "Goodness," "cardinal virtue," and so on. In all these translations, *ren* is understood primarily as an *ethical* concept, just as it has been so taught by the Confucian tradition in China as well as in her neighbors. I differ from any narrowly moralistic interpretation of *ren* in Confucius. Several years ago, I argued in an article[2] that his conception of *ren* was essentially aesthetic. In so doing, I translated *ren* in Confucius simply as "humanness" and interpreted it in terms of human spirituality.[3] Man may be animal-like or be different from all other creatures.[4] For Confucius a man is *truly* human (*ren*)[5] when he is not animal-like. But what is it that makes him "*un*animal-like"? For him it is the presence of human spirituality or sensibility in his being or doing. Confucius teaches various particular virtues such as compassion (*shu*), loyalty (*zhong*), and filial love (*xiao*). For him these are all manifestations of humanness (*ren*) in man's conduct. Along with these virtues, he also teaches the importance of the observance of *li* (ritual/ propriety) in human relations, precisely because he sees the presence of *ren* in such relations. His "noble man" (*junzi*) is indeed a person who recognizes the noble beauty of *ren* and devotes himself to a life of humanness. In one saying (IV, 1), Confucius says: "Recognize beauty (*mei*) in the life of humanness (*li ren*). If one doesn't choose a life of humanness (*chu ren*), how can one be considered to have attained wisdom?"

The character *ren* does appear in pre-Confucian literature, though rarely. When it does, however, it is used basically in the everyday sense of "being kind," as one finds it in Nos. 77 and 103 in the *Shi Jing*."[6] (In both of these two instances, *ren* is used along with another common adjective *mei*, meaning "handsome.") In teaching the beauty of humanness, clearly Confucius introduced a new way of looking at human conduct, that is, in terms of its spiritual meaning.[7] Actions are no longer just what meet our eyes; true human actions are manifestations of humanness in man's conduct. One may say Confucius gave truly human acts their proper names *as specific virtues*. In this sense, I regard Confucius as the discoverer of the human spirit. *Ren* refers to the spiritual dimension of human doing and being.

One may speak of the spiritual side of a human being as the "inner" as opposed to the "outer" aspect of his or her being. However, in Confucius, the "inner" is inseparable from the "outer"; one can speak of the "inner" only as the other side of the "outer," that is, of the visible. In this sense, man's humanness (*ren*) must necessarily be expressed in his visible action or being. Animality implies the absence of the inner. Hence, the saying: "The Master said: 'Ritual [*li*], ritual!' everybody says. But would it mean presents of jade and silk? 'Music [*yue*], music!' everybody says. But would it mean bells and drums?'" (XVII, 11).[8]

Confucius is well-known for his teaching of filial love (*xiao*), one of the cardinal virtues of Confucian tradition. Let us read the following two sayings on this subject:

[A] ZI-YU asked about filial love [*xiao*]. THE MASTER said: "For today's filial sons it means feeding their parents. But don't all do that, including dogs and horses? But they lack respectfulness [*jing*]. Where is the difference?" (II, 7)

[B] ZI-XIA asked about filial love. THE MASTER said: "The hard thing is your look [*se*]. When something is to be done, young people do the job. If they have food and wine, they offer them to the elders. Now, would you consider such a thing filial love? (II, 8)

In [A], the Master implies that the filial son must have "respectful-ness" in his support of his parents. In the absence of this "respectfulness," his care for his parents would be no different from an animal's caring for its parents. Here, one may consider the presence of "respectfulness" as an expression of genuine *human* feeling (*ren*). In [B], Confucius makes it clear that this feeling or humanness is to be expressed in some visible state of being. The basic meaning of the word *se* is "color," and it may also mean broadly the external appearance of a thing. Thus, in this saying, the Master is referring to one's "look" or countenance accompa-nying one's action. The filial son is expected to do whatever he does for his parents *respectfully*. This is the *human* way of serving one's parents. By saying "The hard thing is your look," Confucius is pointing to the diffi-culty of expressing or externalizing one's humanness in one's visible being or action.

2.

As we now turn to Confucius's reading of the *Shi*, I should like to state, at the outset, that for him the experience of the beautiful is uniquely *human* experience in the normative sense of *ren*. In the Introduction, I cited two comments by Confucius on *"Guan Guan, Ospreys,"* one on the song itself, and the other on the musical performance of it by Zhi. Let us recall them.

[A] *"Guan Guan,* Ospreys"[9] is a song of joy free of debauch, sorrow free of hurt. (III, 20)

[B] When the music master Zhi came to the climax of *"Guan Guan,* Ospreys,"* yang yang,* his music flooded my ears! (VIII, 15)

That these two utterances are aesthetic may be evident. In [B] the Master is reporting on his musical experience of the performance. [A] clearly goes beyond the immediate auditory experience. He is remarking on the *beauty* of the song; that is, how it appeals to his aesthetic sense.

Here are two more sayings in the *Analects*, in which Confucius discusses particular Songs.[10]

[A] [In a Song, the poet sings:] "The flowers of the wild cherry flutter and turn./ Not that I don't think of you./ Your house is far

APPENDIX

away." THE MASTER said: "He didn't really think of her. What difference would the distance make?" (IX, 30)

[B] ZI-XIA asked: "[A Song reads:] 'How exquisite her smile dimpling,/ How lovely her clear eyes, so black and white./ You would take her white [su][11] for a flourish.' What is the meaning of this?"

THE MASTER said: "The painting comes after the white."

ZI-XIA: "Ritual [li] comes afterwards?"

THE MASTER said: "You are one who inspires me. With you I can begin to discuss the Shi." (III, 8)

The meaning of [A] may be clear. By saying "What difference would the distance make?" Confucius is commenting on the less than passionate *mind* of this lover, who finds her "too far away." There are different readings of [B]. However, I read it, especially in view of Zi-xia's statement: "Ritual comes afterwards." The Master takes this response to mean that ritual comes *after* the human spirit (*ren*). He thus happily approves of the pupil's understanding.

In another saying (XVII, 10), Confucius tells his son, Boyu, "Have you worked on Zhou Nan and Shao Nan [of the Shi]?[12] A man who has not worked on Zhou Nan and Shao Nan is like one who faces up against a wall." This is obviously a general remark, but significantly, these two chapters belong to *Guo Feng*, like all the other songs mentioned by Confucius that I have referred to. Here I should like to note the fact that Confucius mentions no particular song from any of the other three parts of the *Shi Jing*, namely from *Xiao Ya*, *Da Ya*, and *Song*. Does this reflect Confucius's view of these later parts?

As I have noted in the Preface, these parts include mostly songs related to the dynastic history and legends, which often include episodes of war, conquest, lawlessness, and immorality. I speculate that Confucius's reading of the dynastic songs was different from his reading of the folksongs of *Guo Feng*, which mostly express the spontaneous joys and sorrows of people. In some of the practices or episodes sung in the dynastic songs Confucius must have found the working of the human spirit (*ren*), importantly in the observance of the tradition of *li* (ritual/propriety), and in others the opposite or negation of it. Isn't it possible that these songs/poems too should have served Confucius for the education of the noble man—that is, in cultivation of humanness? Here I recognize this possibility especially in light of Confucius's aesthetic concept of the noble man (*junzi*) as well as his aesthetic idea of *ren*. As pointed out earlier, for Confucius the noble man is a person who sees the noble beauty of *ren* and devotes himself to a life of humanness. The pupil should develop his aversion to the ugliness of animality as much as his love of the beauty of humanness.

Notes to the Appendix

1 As I noted earlier, the title "*Shi Jing*" began to appear only after the designation of the "Five Classics" (*Wu Jing*) during the Han dynasty.

2 "Confucius's Aesthetic Concept of Noble Man: Beyond Moralism," in *Asian Philosophy*, Vol. 16, No. 2 (July 2006), pp. 111–121.

3 I am using the word "spirituality" in its broadest sense, not necessarily religious or ethical; that is, in the sense of the (incorporeal) quality related to the working of the spirit.

4 The reader shouldn't take my use of "man" in this essay as an indication of my "male chauvinism." To use "man" rather than "human being" (in any gender-neutral sense) in discussion of Confucius's teachings is quite accurate, in view of the patriarchal universe of ancient China. But apart from this historical fact, any attempt to make this writing gender-free would have made not only my writing unnecessarily cumbersome but also its reading very awkward.

5 That is, "human" in its *normative* sense, as opposed to "human" in its *descriptive* sense. Note that the Chinese character for "human being" in its biological sense is also pronounced "*ren*," though written differently. This is clearly not coincidental. The *Doctrine of the Mean* attributes to Confucius the statement "*Ren* is being human [*ren zhe ren ye*]." This is a normative assertion. A similar passage appears in the *Mencius* (7B:16).

6 See W.-T. Chan, "The Evolution of the Confucian Concept *Jen*," in *Philosophy East and West*, Vol. 4 (January 1955), pp. 295–296, where Chan discusses briefly the occurrence of *ren* in pre-Confucian literature, including *Shi Jing*, the *Book of Documents* and the *Book of Change*.

7 In one well-known saying, Confucius declares: "I transmit, I do not invent. I am faithful to and love the old way. . . ." (VII, 1) This saying is often cited in support of the traditionalist view that Confucius was merely following the "Way of the Former Kings." On the other hand, some commentators read it merely as the Master's self-effacing statement. I believe neither view is quite correct. True, Confucius did not "invent" a new way. He taught the same "old way," yet he understood it and illuminated it in an entirely new light.

8 In another saying (III, 3), Confucius utters a similar sentence, using a pun-like phrase in Chinese: "A man [*ren*] who is inhuman [*bu ren*], what can he have to do with ritual [*li*]? A man [*ren*] who is inhuman [*bu ren*], what can he have to do with music [*yue*]?"

9 The first song of the *Shi Jing, Guo Feng*.

10 Neither of the two *Songs* cited here is found in the *Shi Jing*.

11 The original meaning of *su* is plain, white silk, before dying.

12 The first two chapters of the *Shi Jing, Guo Feng*.

Bibliography

Classical Sources
(The following two works are commonly cited in later commentaries, including in the recent sources listed below, as "Gu Zhu" (Old Commentary) and as "Xin Zhu" (New Commentary).
Zheng Xuan. *Mao Chuan Zheng Jian*. ("Gu Zhu")
Zhu Xi. *Shi Ji Chuan*. ("Xin Zhu")

Recent Sources in Japanese
(All these titles give the original text of *Shi Jing*, along with Japanese translations and comments.)

Mekada Makoto, trans. *Shikyō · So Ji* (*Shi Jing* and *Chu Ci*) [目加田誠 譯, 『詩經, 楚辭』]. Tokyo: Heibonsha, 1979.
Shirakawa Shizuka, trans. *Shikyō, Kokufū* (*Shi Jing Guo Feng*) [白川靜 譯, 『詩經 國風』]. Tokyo: Heibonsha, 1990.
——, trans. *Shikyō* (*Shi Jing*) [白川靜 譯, 『詩經』]. Tokyo: Chūōkōronsha, 2000.
Takata Shinji, trans. *Shikyō* (*Shi Jing*), 2 volumes. [高田眞治 譯, 『詩經』 (上, 下)]. Tokyo: Shūeisha, 1996.
Yoshikawa Kōjirō. *Shiky , Kokufū* (*Shi Jing Guo Feng*), 2 volumes. [吉川幸次郎 譯, 『詩經 國風』 (上, 下)]. Tokyo: Iwanami Shoten, 1997.

Other References

Edwards, E. D., trans. *Festivals and Songs of Ancient China*. (*Fêtes et chansons anciennes de la chine* by Marcel Granet). New York: Gordon Press, 1975.
Waley, Arthur, trans. *The Book of Songs*. New York: Groves Press, 1960.

Printed and bound by CPI Group (UK) Ltd, Croydon, CR0 4YY

09/06/2025

14685960-0001